Conve.......g
Conversations to
Customers

THE ESSENTIAL GUIDE TO SOCIAL MEDIA SALES
SUCCESS

Nicky Kriel

Dear Rebecca

Here's to profitable conversations

Pentamerous Publishing Ltd

Nicky Kriel

Cover design by David Sewell of Afflatus Ltd
Illustrations by Herve G-Werty
Author Photography by Ingrid Weel Photography

Pentamerous Publishing Ltd
Suite 2, South Street
Farnham, Surrey GU9 7QU
www.pentamerouspublishing.com

Converting Conversations to Customers/ Nicky Kriel. —1st ed.
ISBN 978-0-9955515-0-3

*Dedication to my three greatest achievements; my lovely children
Natasha, Emily, and Peter*

Contents

Foreword

By Tim Hughes, UK Business Development Director at Oracle, and described as an 'Innovator and Pioneer' of Social Selling. He is the author of 'Social Selling—Techniques to Influence Buyers and Changemakers'.

When I first met Nicky, she had just published her first book, 'How to Twitter for Business Success', and this hit the bestseller list. I've always recommended it to people who wanted to use Twitter for personal or business reasons.

Even then, she talked about writing a book focused on using Twitter and LinkedIn for small business. I felt flattered when she asked me to write this foreword.

In a world of Social Media and Digital Marketing, your customers are now doing a significant piece of their customer journey on-line. Most, if not all, customer journeys start on Google. The journey will also often take place in 'salesperson' avoidance mode. So how, as a small business or sole trader, are you going to stand out?

The term Social Selling is often misunderstood. It is seen as selling, but using Social Media. It is not. Social Selling is a new way of working that matches that of the modern, social savvy buyer. But don't think this book is about some 'fluffy' new way of marketing; it is not. The book is clear in its objective that, as a business, you need leads and to close sales. The book never loses sight of this fact. And, using Nicky's techniques in this book, you will be able to do just that: create leads using Social Media.

Nicky has created five steps to provide the reader with structure. Parts of the book are written in a workbook style to allow the reader to work step-by-step. There is also time in each chapter for you to think and reflect on how to apply this to your business.

For example, in the important section on personal branding, Nicky not only spends time walking you through why you need to focus on creating a personal brand to attract customers but also how to optimise your profile.

Buyers want to be educated. If you are buying a car, you may have an idea of the kind of car you want to buy, but you also want to research the options and decide on what is right for you. An article on the top ten things you need to think about when buying a Sports Utility Vehicle (SUV) will be far more attractive than a sales person waving a banner saying, 'Best SUV deals in town.' The article is educational to the buyer and, if used correctly, should take the buyer down a path to the old-fashioned close.

This book will equip the sole trader and small business on how to use Social Media to market and sell in today's connected economy.

Welcome

This book will not show you how to get rich quickly or make six figures in six months. It won't show you how to become a sales machine on Social Media or how to set Social Media on autopilot, spewing out sales messages. Sorry, if you are after that type of book, stop reading right now!

I believe too strongly in the human side of Social Media. There is a reason for the word 'Social' in Social Media. Social Media is not so much about technology, but about people and relationships. Technology enables you to build a far bigger network of people and reach far more people than ever before. Technology is definitely important but, ultimately, people do business with people they know, like, and trust, and no business can survive without sales. If you need help to increase revenue by acquiring more customers and retaining your existing customers, then continue reading. You may even enjoy the journey!

This book shows you a way of using Social Media to increase sales without being salesy. It is not about 'selling' on Social Media but rather about using Social Media to nurture relationships into revenue. It works well for business-to-business markets and businesses that provide a service. It is suitable for businesses where the value of acquiring each new customer and their lifetime value make it worth the time spent building that relationship.

This book will show you how to:

- Build your personal brand so that people feel that they know, like, and trust you
- Help attract the right customers to find you
- Listen for the business opportunities that occur each day on Social Media
- Search for and find new ideal customers so that you can start building relationships
- Make connections to turn strangers into acquaintances and some of them into friends, business partners, advocates, and even customers
- Research your customers to build relationships
- Develop relationships with potential customers through online conversations
- Know when to take the relationship off-line
- Research your potential customers so that you are prepared when you speak to them
- Nurture relationships so that when people are ready to buy, you are top-of-mind, and when you want to have a sales conversation, people will be willing to talk to you
- Convert online relationships into sales
- Maintain relationships with customers after sales
- Measure the results of your Social Media activities

This book will teach you how to use Social Media in such a way that the sales process feels easy and natural. You'll find that sometimes sales will occur directly on Social Media, and sometimes you will attract people who want to work with you, but mostly you will need to be proactive about finding potential customers and building relationships until the time is right to move the conversation off-line.

Converting Conversations to Customers will show you how to sell more without cold calling or feeling salesy. It will also show you that you don't need to spend all day on Social Media, and you don't need a big budget to grow your business.

Who is this book for?

I have written this book for business owners who don't have a sales and marketing department or a big budget. Not everyone reading this book will have a website or sell goods and services online.

In November and December 2013, Hibu and Impact Research conducted 1,800 online interviews with small and medium-sized businesses in the US and the UK. Out of the people they interviewed, only:

- 7.5% of revenue generated by US businesses was online
- 18.6% of revenue generated by UK businesses was online

In September 2015, the UK Government's Department of Business Innovation and Skills published research, which showed that while 98% of small businesses in the UK are online:

- Only 64% have a website
- Only 28% sell goods and services online
- Businesses actively using the internet to promote or sell are almost twice as likely to grow

You don't have to have a website to use Social Media to increase sales, and you don't need to have an e-commerce site to measure the results.

While all Social Media platforms can be used for Social Selling, this book concentrates on the powerful Social Selling duo—LinkedIn and Twitter. These two platforms will give you the best dividends for your time if you can count the number of customers you need to have a successful business.

You don't have to be young or tech-savvy to be able to harness the power of Social Media for your business.

I am not a millennial—my children fit into that category. I didn't grow up with digital; in fact, I missed out on a lot of technology changes by being at home with my children. I stopped working in the corporate world in 1996. I have done things like selling Tupperware (it weighed little, and I was pregnant with my third child at the time). I have helped friends start up businesses from spare rooms in their houses. I retrained as a Master NLP practitioner, and it was to grow my coaching business that I started networking.

I ventured into the Social Media world tentatively in 2009, so I was by no means an early adopter. People I met at networking kept on raving on about Twitter and how good it was for business. So, I set up a Twitter account in August 2009. However, I didn't get it. I didn't understand what was going on and how I could possibly use it for business. So, after a few days, I gave up.

In December that year, I listened to my first ever webinar about Social Media. Investing in Mari Smith's Twitter and Facebook course changed my life. I started on Twitter and had my first business enquiry within a couple of weeks. Doors started opening for me. I attended my first Tweetup at the beginning of 2010, and the ripple effect of meeting those people had a far wider impact than I could have imagined at the time. I got radio and podcast interviews. I set up a new Toastmasters group in Farnham, predominately using Twitter. It chartered nine months after the inaugural meeting.

In 2010, I ran my first training course on Twitter, and from there, trained LinkedIn and Facebook. Since then, I've worked with over a thousand people, either in groups or individually. I've worked with a wonderful variety of businesses, ranging from fetish underwear to electronic companies, from solopreneurs to multinationals, from holistic healers to accountant firms, and even a prince.

When I started out, the question was: Is Social Media a fad? What is Twitter? Is LinkedIn respectable? Isn't Facebook just for friends?

We've moved from that to: How do I get started on Social Media? How do I use Twitter, set up a Facebook Page, use LinkedIn ... ?

If you are still asking: How do I get more followers or Likes on my Facebook page? You are asking the wrong question.

The question that everyone should be asking is:

How can I make sure that Social Media works toward my business objectives?

You cannot ignore Social Media. Microsoft has just bought LinkedIn for a staggering figure. They could have bought it at a fraction of the cost just a few short years ago. They didn't see the relevance of the platform or Social Media. Don't make the same mistake.

I am not interested in using Social Media to follow celebrities or breaking news or political campaigns. I don't care what the increase in selfies means for our society. I care about helping business owners to grow their business by using Social Media effectively. When small businesses grow, they have a positive effect on the local economy.

The purpose of this book is to help make Social Media simple enough for you to take action within your business.

I would love to connect with you on LinkedIn and Twitter if we haven't already. You will find me as Nicky Kriel on LinkedIn and @NickyKriel on Twitter.

If you haven't started on Twitter yet, you are welcome to do my free Twitter mini-course to help you get up and running.

http://www.nickykriel.com/free-twitter-mini-course/

I would love you to send me a picture of you and this book. I've been amazed at how many locations my 'How to Twitter for Business Success' book has visited.

Are you ready to get started?

CHAPTER 1

Social Media and Sales

What is Social Selling?

The term 'Social Selling' is a bit of a buzzword at the moment, but I will use it throughout the book, so it is useful if you have a clear idea what it means. Most things I read about Social Selling seem to be geared toward corporate businesses with sales and marketing departments, but I believe Social Selling is the perfect technique for small business, and even sole traders, to adopt.

Just to clarify things, when I talk about small business in this book, I am using the UK definition of small business as less than 50 employees, rather than the US definition that categorises small business as businesses with less than 500 employees.

In a larger company, marketing and sales tend to fall under different departments. Social Selling would fall under the sales department. The majority of small businesses do not have a sales department. In fact:

- 96% of all UK businesses are classed as micro businesses with nine employees or less
- 62% of all UK business owners are sole proprietors

- Approximately 96% of all US businesses would fall under the micro business category*
- Approximately 75% of all US businesses are non-employer businesses

(*The Statistics of US Businesses for 2013 excludes data on non-employer businesses. I looked at the number of firms employing nine or fewer employees and added the non-employer businesses to work out the percentage of micro businesses in the USA.)

My experience with working with small businesses is that, even if there are a larger number of employees, the decision-makers are often only a handful of people. Small business owners have to take on a number of functions within their company and become a jack-of-all-trades, doing marketing, sales, PR, administration, accounts, and IT, let alone providing the service or product they sell. Even if a business has an allocated sales person or sales people, the responsibility of selling falls firmly on the business owner's shoulders.

No matter how many hats a business owner has to wear, sales is an essential one. No business can survive without revenue.

Social Selling isn't about selling on Social Media, it's about:

- Building relationships so that the sales process flows naturally from conversation
- Attracting customers who want to buy your service or product
- Staying top-of-mind so that when people are ready to buy, you are the obvious choice
- Proactively finding potential customers and treating them like human beings rather than a number
- Being more personal than mass marketing and more humane than treating potential customers as suspects and prospects
- Building your personal brand and providing useful content
- Discovering opportunities and new customers by listening and searching and finding people you want to work with

- Nurturing relationships with both your existing customers and potential customers so that they are ready to buy when the time is right
- Converting connections to customers by taking the online relationship, which has been built by conversations and content offline
- Measuring the effects your Social Media have had on your bottom line so that you can do more of the things that work

Social Selling provides real opportunities for small business owners to build awareness, find new customers, and grow their business without having to become pushy. Great sales people know the benefit of listening to their customers and asking the right questions.

Using Social Media to sell doesn't mean that everything stays online. Face-to-face meetings and telephone calls with your customer are still essential for closing sales.

- It does, however, make the sales process easier and more pleasant for people who don't think of themselves as salespeople
- It can shorten the sales process substantially
- It is so much easier when your customers qualify themselves and approach you to do business
- It is also much easier to approach people for business when you have already established a relationship with them
- It can be done on a shoestring budget

Small businesses are more agile than Corporates and can adapt to new sales opportunities and markets quickly. Social Selling can give business owners a tremendous advantage over their competitors by simply being able to engage with new customers directly. LinkedIn and Twitter tend to be a great combination for Social Selling, especially for business-to-business, but with the right approach, any Social Media platform can be used successfully for Social Selling.

Even if you believe that your customers are not using Social Media, there are enough potential customers already on Social Media to grow your business, and you may even find great people to collaborate with for business and new suppliers.

Why Selling is Natural

EXPERT: STUART MORRIS

I met Stuart Morris when Pop-up Business School invited me to speak at the Henley Business School in the UK. He worked as the lecturer on Entrepreneurship at Henley. Stuart is an avid entrepreneur, trainer of entrepreneurs, teacher, and tech inventor. He has a passion to see people lifted out of poverty by building sustainable businesses, and has been involved in highly successful entrepreneurship projects in Moldova, Kazakhstan, Turkey, and the UK, and is a TEDx speaker. Stuart spoke at my Social Media Summit for Small Business, and I loved what he said so much that I asked if I could interview him for this book. Here is what he had to say about Social Selling:

Social Selling is in our DNA

Human beings are social creatures; we like to exist as groups. Our natural state is to interact with one another, not only for our own good but also for the good of the group. Throughout human history, we have traded, negotiated, and discussed. Selling is, essentially, that. Selling is part of who we are.

- The farmer grows the corn
- The miller buys and grinds it
- The baker buys the flour and bakes it into bread
- We buy the bread

This natural process of the specialisation of the trades is built into our DNA.

Social selling—using Social Media to sell—is simply an extension of that. We've gone from the geographic community to the virtual community, but the concept remains exactly the same.

Trade is fundamental to the way life exists. If you look at symbiotic relationships, you will find lots of examples, just like the bee and the flower can't exist without each other. The difference with human beings is that we negotiate relationships voluntarily. Our ability to give oils the wheels of social interaction.

The selling part is when you agree: You do this for me, and I'll do that for you. There is an explicit transaction. A lot of social interaction is implicit transactions. We're not expecting something back.

Imagine if you walk into the pub, stand at the bar, and say, 'Right, everybody, I would like you to buy my double glazing.' You just know that if you were to do that, everybody in the pub will say, 'Really?', and you are now the least favourite person.

Even if you were to walk into a pub and say, 'Barman, I want to buy everybody a pint. Buy my double glazing,' people will accept the pint but will still feel somewhat suspicious of you.

If you want to sell to a group of people in a pub in a social setting, you need to be part of the community first. You need to have earned the right to be part of the community. Then, when you are at the table with three or four people and one of them asks, 'What do you do?' and you say, 'I sell double glazing,' one of them may say, 'I've been thinking about getting some double glazing.' At this point, you have earned the right to have the conversation.

Being part of the community

Selling on Social Media is the same. We need to be part of the community in order to be trusted and earn the right to talk about what we do and sell.

Your customer has a problem or need of some kind. They may be looking explicitly, like searching online, or they may be looking subconsciously. The customer is looking for benefits. They don't buy features.

When we are on Social Media, we try to find the customers already on the buying journey and focus on them rather than just broadcasting to everybody. We need to say who we are, and what it is we do, but we don't need to throw that in everybody's face the whole time because it's in our LinkedIn Profile and Twitter bio, anyway.

The handshake

The other aspect about Social Selling is the handshake; the moment the deal is done. It's the moment when I choose to trust you.

Whenever we buy something, there is a moment of trust, and the higher the value, the higher that trust needs to be. So, when you are buying a house, for example, you have the surveyor and the solicitor all involved to make sure that this transaction is trustworthy.

When we are Social Selling, we need to build that relationship of trust. Now, if what you are selling is sweets for 5p, it doesn't need much trust. If you are selling a day's consultancy, then (obviously) you have got to build up the relationship with the potential client so that they believe that, on the day, you will deliver that amount of value at least.

There are too many people who just broadcast, 'Hi, I've got stuff for sale.' They have no relationship with you.

Foundation of trust

We don't have to be best friends, but I want to believe that what you try to sell to me is worth it and that you are trustworthy. This is why the Amazon review system and the eBay buyer and seller rating systems are actually important. We look at a seller with a lot of positive feedback, and will buy something from somebody we've never met before, because other people have had a good experience, and so we feel that we can trust them.

For Social Selling, building that foundation of trust is of utmost importance. Building trust isn't just about having a one-on-one conversation. If you blog, post, and tweet regularly on a particular subject, the customer can build trust because they see how you behave online. Your behaviour must be consistent with your message. They can dig around online and see what you're like:

- How you write
- How you think
- How you behave
- How you respond to complaints

When you come to have the one-on-one conversation and are more into the buying process, your potential buyer feels that they know you.

Enable your customer to buy

The best sales are when we enable the customer to buy; so, instead of pushing our sales messages at them, we pull them toward something that they're looking for already. We solve their need.

Selling is about understanding where the customer is in their journey, and what their needs are and the timescale of their needs.

Your successful sale is the point where you are the person they think of at the moment they are ready to place the order. Social Media allows you to be in your client's mind at the moment that they are ready to buy. And it allows you to do that incredibly cheaply.

You have to be intelligent about what the time costs are that you are prepared to spend.

- Think about where your customers hang out, both physically and virtually
- Think about what they're doing when they're hanging out there
- Find them
- What time of day they are online
- What hashtags they are using or looking for

Don't just stand on top of a cliff and shout, because your voice will get lost in the wind.

For small business, getting your head around selling is vital; without sales, your business is dead.

Social Media is just another tool. It's not complex, and it's not particularly difficult. It may just be unfamiliar, and it's worth spending some time doing it. Do whatever it takes to learn how to use it, but it's not rocket science.

We are social creatures, and it's just having a conversation with people.

Thank you, Stuart.

Why LinkedIn and Twitter

While all Social Media platforms can be used for Social Selling, this book concentrates on LinkedIn and Twitter. They tend to have the biggest impact for higher value customers.

Social Media has become part of our way of life. Typical Internet users are now spending over an hour per day on Social Networks. Facebook dominates the Social Media landscape, but not everyone will be approachable for business on Facebook. Many business owners feel uncomfortable about exposing their private life to people and potential customers and don't want to use their Facebook profile as business people, and that's okay.

I am not suggesting that you ignore Facebook or any other Social Network. In fact, most people I interviewed find Facebook useful for networking and finding out more about customers. I connected with people on Facebook, LinkedIn, Twitter, and Instagram, and use these platforms on a daily basis.

Ultimately, Social Selling is a process and not about the platforms. You need to interact with your customers where they hang out, not where you are most comfortable.

At the moment, the platforms where sales people get the best results for generating leads for business are LinkedIn and Twitter. If you market business-to-business or provide a service or have high-price items that you sell, you will find it useful to start by concentrating on the powerful Social Selling duo: LinkedIn and Twitter.

In this book, I provide you with practical how-to guides so that you can roll up your sleeves and take action. LinkedIn and Twitter are easy to use with your business hat firmly in place. And, it's a great place to get started along your Social Selling journey.

Both LinkedIn and Twitter have strengths and weaknesses, but when you use both of them together, they complement each other nicely.

I tend to think of LinkedIn as an earth element. It is consistent, prosperous, reliable, money-orientated, and wise. The negative side of LinkedIn is that some people can see it as boring and stale.

Twitter, on the other hand, I see as water—in particular, a river. It is vibrant, fluid, conversational, full of emotions, compassionate, and fast-flowing. The negative side of Twitter is that it is hard to keep track and can be seen to be fickle.

Formality

On LinkedIn, you are always in business mode, and on Twitter, you are a person who does business. When you use LinkedIn, think of it as wearing a suit and tie. What would you say in a boardroom or a presentation to a new prospect? Everything is about business. Twitter is like going to a familiar networking event where you know a lot of people, or to a local pub. You are aware that you are a businessperson. The people you meet will know what you do, but you show your human side. You connect with people on a personal and emotional level. So it is good to bring up the weather, family, and sports because you want to find people who are like you. It is about social dialogue. Of course, if someone wants to talk to you about business, you do.

Nobody on LinkedIn wants to hear about what you are eating or see pictures of kittens. What they are interested in is talking about business, and they want to know if you are the right person to work with.

Professionalism vs. likeability

LinkedIn is all about professionalism. You show this through providing your experience and skills for anyone to read. You connect with other business people and show your expertise by answering questions relevant to your industry. Everything is available in one place.

Twitter is all about letting people see who you are so that they know, like, and trust you. Your personality comes out in less than 140 characters. People get a flavour not only of your expertise but also how you interact with other people. You let people sample before they buy. For people to get a full picture, they need to go off Twitter to your website, blog, or LinkedIn profile. People get an impression of what you are like over time. On Twitter, remember that you are a businessperson and that what you say also reflects on your business. Do not Tweet drunk or angry!

Brevity vs. expansion

The 140-character limit on Twitter has led to abbreviations and jargon and shortened links. The benefit of the 140-character limit is that people have learnt to be succinct and witty in a sentence. I chuckle away to myself reading some tweets. The disadvantage is that it is easy to be misunderstood, and is not long enough to expand on what you mean. To get into detail, you need to produce a blog article, get someone to call you, or email further information. Since 2015, you now have more space to elaborate in Direct Messages. It is likely that Tweets will be allowed to expand beyond 140 characters in the future.

LinkedIn allows you to elaborate on points and also allows for a more thoughtful and considered response. Discussions are taking place in Groups as well as in response to posts. It also allows you to publish your expansion of your views directly, using LinkedIn Publisher.

> *Tip: Craft your Tweets so that they get your message across clearly. On LinkedIn, remember, just because you have the space to expand, it doesn't mean that you should be verbose.*

Immediacy vs. continuity

Although Tweets are permanently searchable, they are only visible for a moment in time. It is hard to track back to conversations if you have a busy stream. They need to be repeated to allow for their short lifespan. LinkedIn status updates, group discussion, and internal messaging make it easier to elaborate, and it can easily be referred back to. If you ask the same question on Twitter and LinkedIn, after about an hour, nobody is likely to answer the Twitter question, yet you will still get answers on the LinkedIn group discussion days and even weeks later. All these LinkedIn answers are easy to access and refer to even months later.

For immediate feedback, Twitter is brilliant, but for longevity, LinkedIn wins. However, don't underestimate how long people will remember a funny or punchy tweet.

Initiating vs. deepening

Twitter makes it accessible to contact anyone. You can build relationships quickly and, if you are authentic, those relationships will build into real life conversations and working relationships. On Twitter, you can follow anyone you want, and it is easy to begin relationships with people you want to know.

LinkedIn is more formal, and you have to know the person to connect with them, be a member of the same group, or ask someone for an introduction. Not everyone will connect with people that they haven't met. It is, however, great for deepening existing relationships initiated elsewhere. The one advantage LinkedIn has over Twitter is that you can own your contact database; you can download it and keep it.

Both LinkedIn and Twitter are good for building relationships, but you won't build any relationships if you are not proactive about following or connecting with people in the first place. And starting a dialogue with them.

Conversation vs. nurturing

Twitter is chatty and great for conversations. You can chat and interact directly with people in real time. People will often meet virtually at an arranged time for Twitter chats. Twitter's nature is in the moment, which means that, often, conversations don't get followed up because people have been distracted by the next thing. It is hard to track who said what to you a week after the conversation if you interact with a lot of people. LinkedIn is built for nurturing relationships; you can tag people by how you met them. It even has a simple Customer Relationship Management (CRM) built in so that you can add notes about conversations, set alarms to follow-up, and see messages sent between the two of you.

Numbers

LinkedIn has 414 million registered members and is growing two new members a second. Twitter has a slower growth rate but far higher numbers of monthly active users; in fact, over three times the number of monthly active users, with 320 million vs. LinkedIn's 96 million. Over a billion tweets get sent every two days.

LinkedIn is largely untapped because many people sign up to LinkedIn, create a basic profile, and accept the odd invitation to connect, and that's about all they do. The average time that people spend on LinkedIn is 17 minutes a month, and that is because a large number of people don't use LinkedIn on a regular basis. They will set up a profile and then forget about it.

Very few people tap into LinkedIn as a database and networking tool.

Twitter is largely untapped because most business sees it as a tool to broadcast about their business or free advertising. Often, people will set Twitter up on autopilot and leave it.

Very few people take the time to listen for opportunities and build relationships on Twitter.

Search

Both platforms are powerful for search: LinkedIn is better for finding the right people based on job description, keywords, and company. Twitter is better for finding people interested in a topic and for tracking conversations in real time.

LinkedIn boasts the world's largest audience of influential and affluent people. Not all the Forbes 500 CEOs use Social Media, but of those that do, most will be on LinkedIn. Certainly, there are enough business people to do business with you.

According to LinkedIn research, the average household income is $109,000, and 45% of users are decision makers. These are the people who have the buying power, whether they are:

- Directors of the company
- Managers
- Human Resources
- Business owners
- People in charge of purchasing decisions

On LinkedIn, the chances are good that you can talk directly to people who can make a difference to you and can use you. The problem is that many other people might be trying to sell their services to them, and this is where Twitter is incredibly useful. People are more likely to connect with you on LinkedIn if they recognise you from Twitter.

Not everyone with a Twitter account has a LinkedIn account, and not everyone with a LinkedIn account has a Twitter account.

Sometimes, you might find someone on LinkedIn or Twitter, but it will be obvious that they are inactive on both these platforms, and you may have to find them on Facebook or Instagram to interact with them. The key to success, using Social Selling, is to learn the process and adapt it to what works best for your business.

LinkedIn: Free vs. Premium?

Do you need to have a Premium LinkedIn account to find customers and generate sales?

The answer is no.

I am not suggesting that a premium account can't help you, but consider the following:

LinkedIn is probably the most underutilised Social Media platform. The vast majority of people set up a LinkedIn Profile and only use LinkedIn to accept or send connection requests. The last figures that I've seen for time spent on LinkedIn are 17 minutes per month, which is incredibly low. Very few people truly tap into this incredible database, and all the elements of Social Selling can be done within the free version. Professionals within the Sales and Recruitment Industries often use premium versions such as Professional and Sales Navigator because they use LinkedIn proactively and see it as an essential tool for their trade.

- Most small business owners can use the free version to generate sales. Learn how to get the most use out of the free version before you start paying for it. This book is written on the premise you are using the free version

- If you are proactive on LinkedIn and find that the constraints of the free version restrict you, then—and only then—switch over to the premium version

- It may be useful to pay for a month's use of the premium version to use it strategically for a particular reason. A copywriter that I know, used the premium version of LinkedIn for one month only to find and contact his target market. He didn't try to sell when he InMailed them. All he said was that he was sending them a letter in the post with an unusual design on the envelope. His mailing told them about his copywriting skills. He generated £20,000 worth of business

- If you have a premium account and are not using LinkedIn proactively to generate business, you are flushing money down the toilet!

I thought it might be helpful to show you the difference between the free and the premium version at the time of writing this book, and so I have created a table for you.

You can download the table at www.nickykriel.com/freeresources.

Five Keys to Successful Social Selling

Social Selling is using Social Media to increase revenue for your business by:

Attracting potential customers to you by building your personal brand and providing useful content. (We are going to cover this in Part 1 - Attract)

Discovering opportunities and new customers by listening and searching and finding people you want as customers. (We are going to cover this in Part 2 - Discover)

Nurturing relationships with both your existing customers and potential customers so that they are ready to buy when the time is right. (We are going to cover this in Part 3 - Nurture)

Converting connections to customers by taking the online relationship, which has been built by conversations and content, offline. (We are going to cover this in Part 4 - Convert)

Measuring the effects your Social Media have had on your bottom line so that you can do more of the things that work. (We are going to cover this in Part 5 - Measure)

Part 1 - Attract

It's always easier when customers approach you and are ready to buy. In this section, we will look at how to attract the right customers to you through personal branding and content marketing.

CHAPTER 2

Attract with Personal Branding

V isibility creates opportunity: There is no point in being fabulous if you can't be found. Nobody can do business with you unless they are aware you exist and, often, that means a Google search, or that your name gets mentioned on Social Media. Did you know that LinkedIn profiles rank high on Google Search? There is a good chance that if someone is searching for your name, your LinkedIn profile will be one of your top search results. Google also indexes your Twitter account, and individual tweets will pop up in a search too. I've had someone attend one of my courses because he saw a Tweet about it in a Twitter Feed on someone's website. He didn't even have a Twitter account!

WHY IT IS IMPORTANT TO BUILD A STRONG PERSONAL BRAND

It's easier when customers approach you: The lovely thing about building a strong personal brand online is that customers can find you easily, and you'll find that new customers will approach you to do business. Normally, they have prequalified themselves by the time they speak to you. Recent research studies have shown that between70 – 90% of the buying process has already happened before buyers approach the company.

You don't want to put customers off from doing business with you:

If someone is interested in doing business with you, there is a strong chance that they will pay attention to your online presence. They want to know whether they can trust you. Often, it's the small details that put people off. If it looks as though all you do is spam people on Social Media, then that will deter people from connecting. A neglected and dusty Social Media account doesn't make a good impression either. However, if someone sees that you talk to people on Social Media, they can get a feel for what you would be like to work with.

PROFESSIONAL, PERSONAL, AND PRIVATE

Many business owners that I work with feel uncomfortable about creating Social Media profiles in their own name or using their own photos; they would rather hide behind their company logo because:

- They feel vulnerable
- They hate their picture
- They want to appear as though they are a bigger business than they are
- They only want to use Social Media for their business
- They don't want anyone to know about their private life

Maybe, you recognise some of these objections.

Unfortunately, you can't hide behind a corporate logo anymore. People do business with people that they know, like, and trust. It is exceptionally hard to form a relationship with someone online when all you have to go on is a logo and their business name. Nowadays, it is almost impossible to have a distinct 'corporate' and 'personal' profile. It is easy to spot when someone is inauthentic online. Our public and personal lives have merged online.

The most important thing is to know who you are and be consistent across all your accounts. This doesn't mean that you should air your dirty laundry in public. It is good to know where your boundaries are between public, personal, and private. There are strong reasons to share titbits that show your personality because it lets people get to know you on a human-to-human level. Choose which aspects you don't mind sharing, and which aspects you want to keep private. Things that are truly private are best left completely offline. You may also choose to be more formal and business orientated on LinkedIn than you are on Twitter, for example.

The main objective of personal branding is for professional success. You want to establish yourself as an authority in your area of expertise, as well as being likeable and trustworthy. If your personal life conflicts with your business, you need to know your privacy settings across all your Social Media platforms.

TO BUILD YOUR PERSONAL BRAND:

- Optimise your Social Media profiles (I give you a step-by-step guide on how to make the most of your LinkedIn and Twitter profiles in the chapter 'Optimising your Profiles' later in this book)
- Share interesting and relevant content
- Be credible
- Be helpful
- Stand out for the right reasons

It is worth Googling yourself regularly to see what information can be found online about you.

Your personal branding can lead to your business success far more quickly and cost-effectively than advertising.

TOOLS TO REVIEW YOUR PERSONAL BRANDING:

It is always good to review what information is already out there about you and to keep tabs on what people might be saying.

On a regular basis, do a Google search on your name and your business name and see what comes up (use 'Incognito' mode on Chrome so that the search isn't personalised for you based on your search history), and look beyond the first page of search

Set up Google Alerts on your name so that you get emailed when someone mentions your name (this tends to miss a lot because it will only choose articles that rank highly, but is still worth doing)

Set up an alert on Mention.net (this is great for picking up references on public posts on Facebook, Twitter, YouTube, and Blogs)

Set up an alert on TalkWalker.com. You can set this up for different search terms so that you can search on your name and your business name

Go to your Facebook Personal Profile and find the privacy tab (at the time of writing, this was on the top right-hand side). There is an option to view yourself as a stranger would see you. It's worth checking your privacy settings

---

Expert Tips on Building Your Personal Brand

EXPERT: DEE BLICK

I asked bestselling author of small business marketing books, Dee Blick, to share her knowledge about personal branding. Dee's second book, which has been on Amazon's bestselling list since its publication, has recently been translated and published in Chinese.

Two elements in personal branding

Her first bit of advice was that personal branding has two elements:

- Firstly, what we, as the architect, put into place to create emotional connections with our customers and believe our personal brand to be
- Secondly, the brand reality, which is our customers' view of our brand

A vast chasm can exist between the two. Many small businesses only have one or two employees, or are working on their own and, essentially, their personal brand and business brand are the same. How people perceive you as a person will be of the most influence.

Dee describes personal branding as:

'A collection of genuine emotions, attributes, and beliefs that we have at our core that we want to communicate to the people who can influence a purchase, who can buy from us directly, or connect us to others. We convey our personal brand through the actions we take and the messages we transmit through PR and Social Media. We need to ensure that what we believe about ourselves and how we are perceived are managed perfectly, and that starts by building our personal brand and being consistent and clear about it.'

Our actions and deeds on Social Media are part of our personal brand.

Massive opportunity

Dee sees Social Platforms as a massive opportunity to reach and engage with people in an open and private way.

Open and Private?

'Businesses often go onto social platforms under the misconception that we can go on it to sell on it from the word go and, therefore, we look at our personal brand simply as a way to sell our services, which is flawed. We have to look upon it as a diamond and share many facets because people are not coming onto a social platform to be sold to.

'If all you do is promote the sales side of your business, you are presenting a one-dimensional view.

'Look upon going on a Social Media platform as an amazing opportunity to share everything about you and your personal brand in a rounded way that will have an ultimate benefit to everyone who wants to engage with you. When people connect with you, they are hoping to have an amazing experience that is consistent with what they think they know about you.'

Extension of your offline personal branding

This is a way of extending, online, all the great things that people would know about if they met you in person. Dee believes that it is important to respond to everyone kind enough to connect with you no matter what they say to you. She sees many businesses using Social Media in a way that is easy for them rather than interactive and engaging. They spew out the same type of messages to tick a box rather than show that they are open, inclusive, and welcoming.

Think of the longer game

Dee gave a wonderful example of how being less salesy led to her winning one of her biggest clients. A small business owner, who loved her book, contacted her via Twitter and asked if he could have a chat with her. They had a telephone call, and she didn't feel it appropriate to sell her services right then, but instead, asked him if he could put a review of her book on Amazon. They remained in contact on Twitter. A few months later, he joined a larger leasing company as brand director. When they needed a speaker at one of their events, he gave Dee a call. After the event, they contacted her again and told her that they loved what she had said so much that they wanted to put her on a retainer. They are one of her biggest clients now.

'Sometimes, you have to play a longer waiting game until you fill the gap from meeting people to them becoming your customer. The gap you need to fill is trust. Take your selling hat off and put your social hat on, and remember that there may be a prize at the end of it.'

Dee says she feels dismayed to see so many small businesses only selling on Social Media. She says that it's boring and disingenuous. You don't build a relationship by just selling your services.

DEE'S TOP TIPS

Her tips for personal branding are:

- Know what you stand for and how people who buy from you reflect that. Prepare a CV of points that you can justify
- Be honest!
- Decide on which platforms you want to engage
- Think about the kind of content you want to put out there. People want 'how to' information and solutions to their problems online before they are willing to pay, not only because they hope to solve their problem using free stuff, but also because it builds up trust with the provider of the information
- Think about how you will disseminate all the nuggets in your head
- Think about the ways you engage with your customers already, and think about how you can disseminate offline content online
- Be personable. The mundane stuff is popular because you let people into your life
- Think about how you construct the messages that you put out online

Dee says that you need to think about your Tweets as part of your personal branding, and you should spend time crafting your Tweets.

'Don't think Twitter is quick and that you can fire something off in seconds. You can fire half your potential clients in seconds by creating something that is deemed to be offensive, that is misunderstood, or that is full of spelling mistakes.'

Dee recommends that you watch predictive text!

Thank you, Dee.

Exercise: Focus on Your Business

WHAT DO YOU WANT?

Start with the end in mind. There is no point in doing Social Media for the sake of it. It needs to work for your business. This exercise is about focusing on what you want to gain for your business through using Social Media, and (I'm afraid) that requires you to do some work.

Many of you will scan through this and think that you know what your business is about. That's your choice. But, for those of you who take the time to think about the questions, you will find this exercise valuable, and it will help you to:

- Optimise your profile
- Find your customers
- Know which content to post

In the next chapter, we will go through optimising your LinkedIn and Twitter profiles in more detail.

Most of us think we know what we are about, but can you say what your business is about in a clear and succinct way?

It is so important that you know what your business is about before you start promoting yourself via Social Media. So, it is easy to know in your head what your business is about, but your customers aren't mind readers. They will decide whether they want to work with you or not by the image you present to them via Social Media or your website. It is of vital importance to get your message out in a clear way.

Can you answer the following questions in one clear sentence?

- Who are you, or what do you do?
- Who do you help?
- How do you help them?

Take the time to answer the following questions thoroughly. You will use your answers to help you complete your LinkedIn and Twitter profiles. The answers will also help you when you post content and for searches.

Don't worry if your answers to any of the questions are 'I don't know'. The questions are designed to get you thinking; mull them over, and come back to this again and again to develop your thoughts.

> *There is a Focus on your Business' worksheet with space to write your answers at www.nickykriel.com/freeresources*

QUESTIONS

About Your Business

- Where would you like your business to be in 1 – 2 years' time? What does it look, feel, and sound like? What will you be doing? How will it be different? In what way will it be the same?
- What does success mean to you? What are your criteria for success?
- Describe your business in one sentence. Include:
    Who you are or what you are
    Who you help
    How you help

- What keyword(s) are important for your industry, your location, or your business? (List 10)
- What words or phrases would your customers use to find you, your business, your products, or your services? It is so easy to get lost in our industry's jargon and forget that your customers use different words to describe your product or service, and you need to think in the way your customer thinks
- Why are you using Social Media? ('Because everyone else is doing it' is a weak answer)
- In what way will this help your business?
- What's the one thing that makes you special? Can you say it in one word? Use a maximum of three words to answer this question—ideally, one
- Why should anyone buy from you rather than your competitor?
- How will you know if you are successful at using Social Media?
- How will you measure your Social Media success? (We will cover measuring Social Media in more depth later. For now, use your own words)

About Your Customers

- Who is your ideal customer? What do you know about them in terms of their demographic (e.g., age, gender, etc.), the way they think, and where they are? Do they have particular characteristics? You may have distinct groups of people you want to reach. It's worth listing these groups separately
- Here are some ways of describing your ideal customer (not all of these will be appropriate to your business):
  Male/Female
  Age
  Location
  Job Description
  Size of business

> Value of the business
> Business stage
> Customer lifestyle
> Life stage
> Emotional state
> Need
> Personality
> Likes/Dislikes
> Interests

- What is the problem you are solving for your customer?
- Write down which type of customers you would like to find on Social Media
- Who are they?
- What are they likely to be doing?
- Where do you think they might be hanging out?
- Which people would be useful for you to develop a relationship with?

> Bloggers
> Journalists
> Influencers or Thought Leaders
> Investors
> Advisors/mentors/experts
> Potential customers
> Existing customers
> Suppliers
> Collaborators
> Peers in your industry
> Other

- How do you, or could you, group the customers you currently have?

Work Process

- How do you track people from initial enquiry through to their first purchase? Do you use tools like a contact list? To do lists? Keep it in your head? Spreadsheets? Do you use a Customer Relationship Management system (CRM)?
- How do you follow through with customers once they've made a purchase?
- What are you doing to keep the customers you currently have?
- How do you deal with complaints or problems your customers have?

Value of Your Customers to Your Business

- How many people have you done business with in the past year?
- Are most of your sales one-off purchases or repeat purchases?
- What is the accumulated value of each of your customers since you started doing business with them?
- Look at your top customers:
    - What percentage of your total turnover?
    - What are the characteristics of these customers?
    - How long, on average, do customers stay with you?
    - How often do they buy from you?
- What is the current value of acquiring a new customer to your business?
- How many customers do you need per year?

Why You Need to Optimise Your Profiles

Most people who meet you will never know the full extent of your expertise because they only see a small snapshot of what you do and don't know what you might be capable of doing. If you had to sit someone down and go through all your work experiences and skills, you would probably put them to sleep or put yourself to sleep repeating the same story over and over again to each person you meet.

LinkedIn allows you to put a large amount of information down in one place. If someone is interested in you after they have met you, or is looking for people with your skills and expertise, LinkedIn is an obvious place to go for research. Make sure that your profile showcases you for all the right reasons. Think of your profile as your online Curriculum Vitae (CV) for business prospects and partnerships.

It's lovely when people approach you to work with them rather having to go out and get leads all the time. I can't stress how important it is to fill in all experiences even if you only end up using LinkedIn passively.

Take the time to fill in your LinkedIn profile fully

If someone were to view your LinkedIn account today, what impression would they have of you? LinkedIn is not the most intuitive site to use, and you may hate filling in forms. If you are wondering if it is worthwhile taking the time, here are five reasons to spend time completing your LinkedIn profile:

- LinkedIn ranks highly on search engines. If you Google your name, your LinkedIn account is likely to be one of the first places your name appears. What will someone think if your LinkedIn profile is the first and only thing that they look at?
- People are searching on LinkedIn for potential business partners, services, or suppliers: Can they find you?

- LinkedIn offers you a great opportunity to showcase all your skills and experience. You don't have to repeat the same information over and over to different people
- You don't have enough time to tell people you meet through networking about all your expertise; LinkedIn allows people to find out more about you if they are interested. It may take some time to do it properly, but once it is done, you have all the information in one place
- LinkedIn tries to connect you with people you might know, so when you fill in your past experiences, LinkedIn will suggest people to you who have worked at the same companies at the same time or went to university with you

It is just as important to optimise your Twitter account

Just because Twitter doesn't have much space to display your expertise, doesn't mean that you can afford to ignore your personal branding on Twitter. Your Twitter bio and Tweets are indexed on Google. Make sure you use every available place for personal branding. You may only have 160 characters for your bio, but your personality comes across in your Tweets. People get to know you 140 characters at a time in bite-sized pieces.

How to Optimise Your LinkedIn Profile

DEMONSTRATE YOUR EXPERTISE IN YOUR NICHE

LinkedIn allows you to show your expertise by:

- Having your level of experience available for everyone to see on your profile. It is so important to fill in your profile thoroughly
- By actively taking part in discussions in Groups, you can display your knowledge by giving helpful advice and asking thought-provoking questions
- By providing useful, relevant content as status updates, you show that you take a keen interest in your industry, and it keeps you top-of-mind
- By sharing your blog so that you show your depth of knowledge
- By publishing on LinkedIn, you show your thought-leadership
- By adding rich media to your profile, such as SlideShare, YouTube, and pictures, you make your profile more interesting

Even if you do nothing on LinkedIn but optimise your profile, there is a good chance that you will generate business by being found by the right person who wants to do business with you. I ended up flying to the UAE and working for a Prince in 2014, based solely on my LinkedIn profile. It is always great when work comes in to you without having to actively go out to seek it.

First impressions count. In this section, we will go into depth about all the elements that make your profile complete:

1. Why your photo is important
2. What makes your profile complete
3. Make your profile keyword rich
4. How to improve your headline
5. What to say in your summary
6. Tips for filling in your past and present experiences

7. Showcase your skills with endorsements
8. Recommendations are to be recommended
9. Your banner
10. Other ways to optimise your profile

> *If you would like to use a LinkedIn Profile Checklist as you go along, you will find one at:*
>
> *http://www.nickykriel.com/freeresources*

#1 Why Your Photo is Important

There is no excuse in this day and age of digital photography, where almost everyone has the ability to take pictures with their phones, for not having a picture on LinkedIn. No picture on a profile signals to other people that you are not an active LinkedIn user; that you may have set up a profile at some point, but then lost interest. Our brains are hard-wired to look at people's faces.

Mistakes that people make with their LinkedIn pictures

- No picture
- Obviously dated.—You may like that photo taken over a decade ago, but guess what? Most people can spot that it is not up-to-date
- More than one person in the picture.—Which person's profile is it anyway?
- Obviously cropped from a holiday picture or black-tie event.—It is a professional networking site; don't you have time to get a professional picture taken?
- Non-recognisable picture.—The camera does lie. It captures a microsecond of your facial expressions, and it may not be a true representation of how other people see you. I have had

invitations from people that looked completely unfamiliar to me, but their name rang a bell When I looked closely at their profile, I realised that I knew them even though their photo didn't help

- Fun, casual pictures.—This is LinkedIn, not Facebook or a dating site
- Blurry picture and bad lighting.—Really?!
- Pictures with more than your head and shoulders. The pictures on LinkedIn are small thumbnails, and when people do searches, you want to make it easy for them to recognise you
- Photos on their side.—Yes, I have seen some of these. Some people show they need basic computer training. If you need help uploading a photograph, most teenagers can show you how to do it
- A logo.—Profiles need photographs; save your logo for your company page
- A picture of you from the side, or doing something like looking at your laptop, doesn't make it easy for other people to recognise you

Ideally, you want to have a professionally taken photograph that shows your face clearly. A simple head and shoulder picture works where you look approachable. It doesn't have to be formal, especially if you do something practical or physical, but it should look as though you care enough about your professional branding to make the effort to have a decent picture. If you want to be taken seriously, you need to be serious about your image.

#2 What Makes Your Profile Complete?

- A current position (you can add multiple positions if you wear a few hats like many small business owners I know)
- Two past positions
- Education

- Profile summary (who you are, who you help, and how you help them)
- A profile photo (professional-looking head and shoulder picture)
- Skills (LinkedIn will add ones from your profile automatically, but you will need to check and add to the list)
- At least three recommendations

Check your Profile Strength according to LinkedIn. The highest level you can get to is All-Star, and I am with you if you think that the small gap at the top is misleading.

#3 Make Your Profile Keyword Rich

Your LinkedIn profile features prominently when people do searches for your name, and within LinkedIn, people are continuously searching for someone like you. In order to be found, you need to make sure you add your keywords so that the right people can find you. Think about the words that people who need your service might be searching for, rather than the Industry-specific jargon that you might use.

There are certain places in your profile that keywords get picked up for search:

- Your Name (please, don't add keywords here)
- Your Headline
- Current Experience, including descriptions
- Past Experience, including descriptions
- Summary
- Recommendations

So, make sure you add the obvious words in these places. Often, we know what we do, so we assume that everyone else does too, but you need to state the obvious. Remember, your potential customer is not a mind reader.

Further places that may help with your SEO:

- Skills
- Names of LinkedIn Groups you join

> *Warning: Keyword stuffing (overuse of keywords for the sake of SEO) does not look professional, and may turn off potential customers.*

#4 How to Improve Your Headline

Have you ever had the experience of listening to someone's one-minute pitch at a networking meeting and, when they sit down, you have no idea what they do?

On LinkedIn, you have 120 characters to get your message across.

Your headline on your LinkedIn profile is the most prominent feature of your profile. So, when last did you look at what your headline says about you? Or, is it still set to the default setting and showing your current position and company name?

Why your Headline is important

- Highly prominent on search results when people search for your services on LinkedIn
- Keywords in your Headline are picked up in LinkedIn Search
- Your Headline acts like your sales pitch, enticing someone to read more about you
- Your LinkedIn Headline appears in Google search results if someone searches for your name

- Your Headline may be the only thing on your Profile that your potential customer sees about you

How to make your 120 characters count

Make sure you tell people, in a clear, succinct way:

- Who you are or what you do
- Who you help
- How you help them

Be specific about the type of business or person you work with. The person reading your Headline needs to know at a glance that you are the right person for them.

Think of your keywords

What would other people look for if they searched for your business? Do you believe anyone would look for hackneyed phrases like 'problem solver' or 'blue-sky thinker'?

Be memorable with your Headline

Think of it as your personal brand statement, where you can showcase your specialist area, your value propositions, and what makes you special.

> *Note—don't waste precious space in your Headline with your business name unless it is exceptionally well known. If someone were searching for your business name, your name would appear in the search results anyway because it is in your current position.*

If you haven't reviewed your LinkedIn profile in the last few months, have a look at it now. Does it show you in the best possible light?

#5 What to Say in Your Summary

Do not leave your summary section blank; you are given a wonderful opportunity to use 2000 characters to make your profile irresistible. You don't have to write an essay, but it is worth spending time on this section. You only get one chance to make a first impression. Here are some pointers to help you fill in this section:

Your summary is not about you. I know that may sound contradictory, but when you write your summary, you need to write it for the person who will read it. They want to know whether you can help them or whether they can refer you to someone. So, have your potential customer in mind when you write.

You want to say:

- Who (or what) you are
- Who you help (be specific)
- How you help them

You have an opportunity to go into specific detail about how you help people.

This mind-set helps you to write for your customer and focus on the benefits you offer them rather than the features of your business or expertise.

On LinkedIn, your summary is best written in first person. Biographies have historically been written in third person, but this is not the norm for writing your summary on LinkedIn. The person reading it knows you wrote it, and it is always odd when profiles are written in third person.

Like all good stories, your summary should have an introduction, middle, and conclusion.

In the introduction: You want to say who you are, whom you help, and how you help them in a succinct way so that the person reading it gets drawn in to find out more.

In the middle: You can elaborate about how you help different groups of customers. It is worth telling a story about how there was a problem, the action you took, and the result.

In the conclusion: You want a call to action such as:

- What do you want the reader to do when they've finished reading?
- Let people know what type of people you would like to contact
- Tell people how to contact you

You can also break up the middle section from being just a block of text with heading and subheadings and lists. I have also seen people use lines in their summary section to create powerful headings.

I have used the following phrases, written in capital letters, to act as headlines:

- WHAT I DO
- HOW I DO IT
- WHY IT WORKS

LinkedIn produces a list of the most overused buzzwords each year, and 2015's words were:

- Motivated
- Creative
- Enthusiastic
- Track record
- Passionate
- Successful

- Driven
- Leadership
- Strategic
- Extensive experience

Do you have any of these words in your LinkedIn Profile?

#6 Tips for Filling in Your Current and Past Experiences

- Always fill in your past experience with your future in mind
- You are only selecting a few parts of your past, so think about how your past skills, experiences, and learning can showcase your current ability to be the best person for your potential customers to work with
- Be truthful, but that doesn't mean you have to use the exact words that your employer gave you in the past
- Think of the best way possible to describe your title to include keywords that people might use for search
- A vague title like 'Manager' doesn't help people know what you do/did; add descriptive words that add to your title to help your reader understand your role
- Job titles change over time; make sure you update your positions to be current
- Job descriptions should be creative, descriptive, and succinct
- Your job description will become easier to scan if you use a wide variety of relevant keywords in bullet point
- Use the parts of your history that will enhance your current position

7 Showcase Your Skills with Endorsements

LinkedIn will guess what your skills are based on what you have put in your profile. Make sure the skills are the best ones for you. It is of vital importance that you make sure you add the most appropriate skills to your profile. Why?

It allows people to see your skills at a glance—most people will scan through your LinkedIn profile, and a list of relevant skills shows people they have found the right person.

LinkedIn ranks people they consider influential for a particular skill even though skills don't seem to be found by LinkedIn keyword search yet. I suspect that this ranking continues behind the scenes. There is also a good chance that skills that have endorsements will be relevant in the future.

People can endorse your skills. If you don't have the relevant skills listed, you may be missing out. Skills is the only area, other than recommendation, where social proof works on LinkedIn. Everyone knows that you have written the content for your profile. Even though endorsements are a bit superficial, think about it—if someone says they have a skill, and only one person has endorsed them for it, would you choose them or someone who has fifty endorsements for the same skill?

It is easier to add an endorsement than to give a written testimonial, and so your customers are more likely to do it.

Quick word about endorsements:

When I'm running LinkedIn Workshops, I have found that when we start talking about endorsements, it raises a lot of emotions and questions:

- Yes, people you don't know will endorse you for skills that they don't know you have
- Yes, people will endorse you for skills you don't have

- Yes, people are using it in a spammy way to get attention
- Yes, having endorsements doesn't mean that a person has those skills
- Yes, you need to treat endorsements with a pinch of scepticism
- No, you don't have to endorse people back
- No, you don't have to accept skills that you don't have
- You can't control other people's behaviour, but you can control what you do. Don't worry about what other people are doing. They may have had bad advice, or maybe they clicked on more skills than they intended
- Don't endorse people unless you know they have those skills
- Do use endorsements in a positive way to support people you know have skills
- Do use endorsements to remind people that you are thinking about them
- Do use endorsements to thank people
- Do learn from the endorsements that other people give you—it shows you how they perceive you

I hope that has answered most of your questions about endorsements.

Make sure you receive endorsements

Make sure you list all your skills that your customers would use. You can have up to 50, and I would recommend you add all the ones that are relevant. Use the drop down list when you go to add a new skill to ensure that you are using terminology that your industry uses.

Move your skills section higher up in your profile (all you need to do is to click on the panel bar and drag it higher). This makes your skills more visible and easier to endorse.

Endorse other people first. There is a good chance they will feel positive toward you because you have done something nice without being asked. Most people will endorse you back for your skills.

Things you can do within the edit skills function

- Did you know that you can switch off the endorsement feature on your profile? (Not recommended!)
- Did you know that you can switch off the recommendation that LinkedIn suggests to you?
- Did you know that you can switch off email notification each time someone endorses you?
- Did you know that you can add and delete skills?
- Did you know that you can move skills around? LinkedIn only shows a certain number of skills (so, moving them is useful if you want particular ones to be displayed from the others)
- Learn how to 'manage your endorsements' by playing around in the edit section of skills.

> *Tip: Encourage Endorsements—there s a chance that it may help with SEO, but it definitely helps your credibility. Give endorsements to people that you know have the skills.*

#8 Recommendations are to be Recommended

Recommendations are far more powerful than endorsements because endorsements are just a click of a button, whereas recommendations require a lot more thought.

The quickest tip for getting a recommendation is to give one first

When you recommend somebody, and they go to accept that recommendation, LinkedIn will ask them if they want to recommend you. So, LinkedIn encourages people to recommend you back by prompting them. Obviously, they can say no because, sometimes, it might not be relevant.

However, don't always give recommendations expecting one back. It makes the person you recommend feel good and think positively about you. Plus, other people see you giving recommendations in their news feed, and it keeps you top-of-mind. You never know, it may prompt them to recommend you.

The second best way is to ask for it

Very often, we do work that people would happily give us a testimonial for, but we don't get one because we are too shy/ insecure/ busy to ask for a recommendation. I know because I rarely ask people for recommendations or to endorse me, or to put their kind words into writing. Sometimes, people have already given recommendations for you but they were in an email, or you've used their testimonial on your website.

Make it easy for people to recommend you

The easiest way to get someone to recommend you on LinkedIn is to copy and paste what he or she has already said about you when you ask them for the recommendation. All they need to do is take what they have said already and give it back to you on LinkedIn.

Quite often, people will want to recommend you, but life gets in the way. It is low down on the list of priority versus firefighting and everything else that is going on with their lives and businesses. Often, people want to be thoughtful about what to say, and it puts them off automatically giving the recommendation straight away because they think they will do it when they have a bit more time. And then it gets forgotten about.

Don't let your recommendations get dusty

It is amazing how quickly time can pass. Make sure that your last recommendation is within six months. It doesn't look good if nobody has recommended you for years. Personally, I would be a bit suspicious if nobody recommended you for a few years.

Get in the habit of asking for and giving recommendations

How long would it take to write a quick recommendation for someone you have worked with recently or in the past year? How long would it take to ask the last person you worked with for a recommendation? Or someone that you know was delighted by your service? Why not commit to writing a LinkedIn Recommendation once a month or once a week if you are super-keen? You never know what might come out of it.

> *Tip: Get More than 10 Recommendations—LinkedIn would like you to have at least three testimonials, but don't stop at the bare minimum. Your recommendations are searchable for keywords, so the more recommendations you have, the more chance that they will include keywords that your potential customers are using.*

#9 Your Banner or LinkedIn Background

You have a great opportunity to use your LinkedIn background as, in effect, free advertising space to visually sell or tell more about your story. Here are some ideas for your banner. This can be changed easily:

- Show your products
- Show your team or office
- Show an event/celebration/milestone
- Show you in action
- Show behind the scenes

- Show your branding with your logo and a tagline
- Promote an upcoming event or promotion
- Use an image to convey a mood for your business
- Your contact details

> **Tip:** *I recommend that you use Canva.com if you are thinking of creating an image yourself because Canva has the dimensions for most Social Media images and has templates for layouts to make your work look professional. They also have free and affordable images that you can use.*

#10 Other Ways to Optimise Your Profile

- *Customise your website links.*—You have an opportunity to have three website links in your contact information. Choosing 'Company Website' will not enhance search; choose 'Other'. This option allows you to add a keyword rich and relevant description. Let people know where the link will take them
- *Maximise the number of groups you join.*—The more groups you join, the more potential connections you will have. The names of the groups you join are added to your profile. The keywords in the group names may also be searched
- *Connecting to everyone you know* and some you don't know.—I won't recommend that you connect with every random person who asks you to connect, or that you should ask a thousand strangers to connect, but every person you are connected with potentially helps you get found by their connections. I have had exciting offers come through people that I didn't know before I connected with them on LinkedIn. If you went to a networking event, would you only talk to people you know already?
- *Customise your profile's URL.*—Check what your LinkedIn Profile is at the moment. If it contains a string of letters, it hasn't been customized yet.

- *Set your profile to display all information.*—You want to be found, don't you?
- *Regularly check your profile.*—To make sure it is up-to-date
- *Regularly post updates* that showcase your expertise. This can be either your content or other people's content
- *Use LinkedIn Publisher.*—We will go into this in more detail when we look at content
- *Add rich media to your profile.*—Such as photos, publications, SlideShare, and videos. Did you know that you can? They add an extra dimension to your profile
- *SlideShare.*—This is a sharing platform for presentations. LinkedIn owns SlideShare. Most businesses could put together a presentation about their business, products, or skills on PowerPoint without too much hassle. A SlideShare presentation can be viewed without leaving LinkedIn; plus, you have the bonus that the content can be found on SlideShare as well. More later
- *Video.*—If you have any videos about you or your business, they allow people to hear, see, and get a feeling about who you are far better than copious amounts of copy
- *Interact with other people.*—You can like and comment on other people's posts, and you can also tag connections so that they will know that you've mentioned them. Add the @ symbol before your connection's name and select them from the drop-down menu. This helps people to remember you

How to Optimise Your Twitter Profile

If you have a Twitter account, you have to make sure that when people look at it, they want to follow, connect, or talk to you. As well as putting out good content, you want to attract other people to you by what they find on your profile.

The first element is your personal branding, which a lot of people struggle with on Twitter because they feel vulnerable exposing themselves on a public platform. Quite often, people only show their logo and their business name while their Tweets are all business related, which is fine if you just want bland robots to follow you. More people will connect with people, and showing that you are human is a great way to start a relationship. The one advantage of being a small business is that who you are, makes you unique; therefore, don't feel scared of putting a little bit of your personality online. I'm not suggesting you air your dirty laundry in public, but I do suggest that you allow a little of yourself to ebb through on Twitter so that people can relate to you. As the saying goes, 'Be yourself; everybody else is already taken.'

If you want people to connect with you, it is easier to do business with those that are like you, and you can tell a lot in 140 characters, and your personality does come through—if you allow yourself to be you, not warts and all but the best parts of you. The social element of how you relate to other people shows other people who you are as a person.

'Today, you are you; that is truer than true. There is no one alive who is youer than you.' Dr Seuss

Twitter doesn't have as much space to show your expertise, but make sure you check all these areas within your profile for personal branding opportunities:

1.   Profile picture
2.   What to write in your bio

3. Banner
4. Twitter name and username
5. Link to website
6. Photos
7. Pinned posts
8. Tweets
9. Location
10. Following/Follower ratio
11. Two things not to do (that affect visibility)

#1 Profile Pictures

People do business with people that they know, like, and trust. So, how do you do this on Twitter? Firstly, a profile picture is the part of your branding that people see straight away. Photos of people work, and some much better than pictures of logos. There may be a reason you want to have a logo there, but people connect with people, and eyes connect with eyes.

A head and shoulder photograph, with a smile, and where you look approachable and recognisable is great. Ideally, a picture of yourself will have your eyes pointing toward your Tweets because we instinctively look in the direction that someone else is looking.

#2 What to Write in Your Bio

When you set up your Twitter Profile, how much thought did you put into your bio? Maybe you filled in a few words and planned to come back to it later? When was the last time you looked at what your Twitter profile says about you and your business? Your bio is 160 characters. You don't want it to be a sales pitch because, if you make it too sales pitchy, people will think you will spam them. Put some part of your character in there and make sure it includes the keywords that you want to be known for. After reading this, go and check your bio and see which words are there. Have you included keywords? Have a look at the content of your bio and think that, if you weren't yourself, would you want to connect with you? So many people do not fill in their bio, or they have a bland one.

Here's why you need to put a bit of thought into how you write your Twitter bio:

- **Your Twitter bio is searchable**: Did you know that your bio appears in Google searches? Search Engines will search for keywords within your bio. How many of your keywords (or keyword phrases) for your business are in your bio at the moment? Change your bio every few months just to keep it fresh. I believe, but I don't know for a fact, that as it's Google indexed, it is seen as fresh content by search engines. But even if it isn't, it is good to see if you can tweak it to make it work even better for you

- **People search on Twitter**: People use keywords when they are looking for people to follow. Twitter will suggest tweets and people relevant to the search. Are you likely to get found on Twitter for your keywords? Remember: Use words that people are likely to use when they are searching for your service or product rather than industry jargon

- **Twitter suggests people to follow**: Twitter recommends people to follow based not only on who you follow and are following but also by the words used in your bio. How will Twitter know unless you use the right words?

Your bio may be stopping people from following you

Unless you are a celebrity or a household name, people will not follow people without a bio. Incomplete accounts, or badly filled in bios, put people off from following: Would you follow an 'egg' with no bio filled in? Thought not! Make sure your bio shows a true reflection of who you are, and that you are not putting your customers off. You need to give people a reason to follow you, and what you say in your bio will make the difference to whether people follow you back or not.

Here are some other things that may be stopping people:

- **You don't give enough information**: About who you are and what you do—don't make people guess that you are worth following
- **Your bio is a sales pitch**: Most people do not like being sold to. They may think that you are going to spam them
- **Your bio is so kittens and rainbows**: Okay, if you are just tweeting for fun, it is all right. But, if you are using Twitter to grow your business, you need to tell people about your business and what you will be tweeting about
- **Your bio lacks any personality**: People want to feel that they are talking to a real-life person, not a company logo
- **Your bio is full of corporate mumbo jumbo**: Have you ever been at a networking meeting and heard someone deliver their sixty-second pitch and still been in the dark when they sat down? Avoid language that appears to be generated by a committee. Speak in the language your customer uses
- **Spelling mistakes**: You may not feel it's important, but it may be putting off your potential customers
- **Full of #hashtags**: This seems to be a recent trend, but I think it looks spammy and sends out a message that you are more

interested in Twitter search engines than the person reading your bio

Your Twitter bio should encourage the right people to follow you and also include your keywords.

#3 Banner or Twitter Header

Not everyone will see your Twitter header or banner because most people will view your Twitter profile from an app, but if they use Twitter.com, you have a great opportunity for free advertising space. In addition to the ideas for banners in the 'Optimising your LinkedIn Profile' section, here are more ideas:

- Show something more personal so that people can connect with you on a human level
- Show a hashtag or Twitter chat that you run
- Create a collage to show your personality
- Use one of your own images
- Show a recognisable landmark if you are a local business

#4 Twitter Name and Username

If someone has met you and they look up your name on Twitter, you want them to find you. The only way they will find you is if you include your name in your Twitter name or username (or your bio). It is hard to form a relationship with someone when you don't know his or her name. You can change your Twitter name and username at any time, but it is easier to do (and causes less confusion) when you have few followers.

#5 Link to Website

I'm surprised that some profiles don't include a link to a website. If you don't have a website for any reason, use your LinkedIn profile as your website. Another mistake that I have seen is a link directing people to a landing page, where you try to force people to give you their email address because it is the only option on the page. Not a great way to start a relationship.

#6 Photos and Videos

Your most recent photographs and videos are visible on your profile. Images get 62% more engagement and 82% more retweets than straight text. Twitter is becoming a lot more visual, so you need to include photographs or pictures in your Tweets.

#7 Pinned Posts

You can pin a Tweet to your profile, and I suggest that you pin a Tweet that fits in with your business objectives. At the bottom of any of your Tweets, will be three dots, which when clicked on, will show you the pinning option. Your pinned Tweet can be your sales pitch, a link to your course, or a link to your sales page, etc. The pinned Tweet will be the most visible thing in your profile, so make sure that whatever you pin, it's something positive about your business, or leads to a link to your website. We will talk about Twitter Lead Generation Cards later in the book. (This is a Tweet that allows you to add people to your email list directly from Twitter. A pinned post is an ideal place for it.)

#8 Tweets

People will scan your most recent Tweets to see what type of content you are Tweeting about. Every now and then, it is useful to audit your last few Tweets. Make sure that some Tweets you put out are informative, interesting, and friendly. Things about your feed that will put people off from following you are:

- **No conversations** and interactions with other people

- **Bland**, vanilla type tweets

- **Inactive Account**. Many businesses think they have a Twitter account because their web guy set one up for them, and they have a link to it from their website, and then they wonder why nobody is following them. Small businesses fall into the trap because they don't understand that Twitter involves communicating and being active. I would suggest that, if you have an inactive account for your business, it might be better not to have one. It doesn't reflect well on your business if you have a dusty Twitter account, and it is unlikely that anyone will follow it

- **Every tweet has a link**. Most people don't like being sold to, and a Twitter account with only links suggests automation and an account that is merely broadcasting rather than willing to communicate with people

CHAPTER 3

Attract the Right Customers with Content

I could write a whole tome on Content Marketing for business, but for the sake of this book, I want to keep this section focused on using content to:

- Show thought leadership
- Show your expertise in your industry
- Build relationships with people
- Generate leads
- Help people to buy by answering questions

And doing this as quickly and painlessly as possible.

You need to understand that you do need content

In an ideal world, to become an authority in your niche, you need to create content and share it with your community. Content can be anything from a status update, a picture, meme, blog, video, infographic, or podcast.

However, the reality for most small businesses means that you won't have the time, the resources, or the skills to create enough of your own content. Don't worry, though, as curating and sharing other people's content works well, too, for showing your thought leadership and building relationships.

We will look at:

- How to create a simple content marketing plan to save you time
- How to create content quickly
- How to become great at curating content so that you have a great source of quality content to share easily with your potential customer
- How to build relationships with people with content
- Tools that can help you

If you have never produced any content, start by sharing other people's content and add value by making a brief comment about what you're sharing.

Even if you don't have a website, you can still create and publish content on LinkedIn.

If you are starting out, it is worth spending a bit of time looking for suitable content to post. Look at what resources you have already and collect ideas so that you can plan your content posting.

There is no point in creating or sharing content randomly. All your content should help your customers. Of course, it is all right to sell on Social Media, but you are not going to get too far if all you deliver is 'buy from me' content. You earn the right to sell or promote your business by being a helpful, trusted member of your community. I like to think of it in the ratio that no more than 1 in 5 of your messages should be for blowing your own trumpet.

For example, a good ratio of content:

1. Share content that your ideal customer would find useful—whether it is yours or other people's content

2. Share content that shows you are an expert in your field—such as useful tips or latest industry news

3. Share other people's content—acknowledge and thank them (this helps build relationships)

4. Engage—have conversations with no strings attached, just to get to know the other person better

5. About your business—use customer testimonials, say what you are up to in a business context, make humble brags, offer promotions, events, company news, etc.

The type of content you share on Social Media will need to fulfil at least one of these:

- Is it educational?—Will it help your customer?
- Is it enriching or inspiring?—People remember how you make them feel
- Is it entertaining?—If you can make someone smile, they associate that warm fuzzy feeling with you
- Is it engaging?—Does it encourage interaction?

Everything is becoming more visually focused, so it is useful to check that you have a good blend of formats:

- Text
- Blog articles
- Pictures
- Videos
- And, don't forget audio

TIPS FOR GETTING STARTED

Look at the following:

- What content you have created already; i.e., copy on your website, marketing literature, blog posts, videos, pictures, and presentations

- What content you can create easily; e.g., a list of one-line tips
- What questions your potential customers always ask, and that send you into auto-pilot because you answer it so often (if you can't think of anything right away, it doesn't matter, but pay attention the next time you have an enquiry, or you find yourself going into auto-pilot, and write it down)
- What industry news or blogs you have read already that might be useful to share with your customers
- Google a question you think your customer might ask if they felt ready to buy from you. See what comes up in search results. Do they spark any ideas?

Creating and Planning Content Quickly and Easily

EXPERT: PETER SPRINGETT

I interviewed my friend, Peter Springett, about Content Marketing. Peter is the founder of Bright Content, a business dedicated to helping clients maximize the reach and value of their content through Social Media and employee advocacy. He has led content teams serving some of the biggest global names in the technology industry. He said that he likes to think of Content Marketing as a cycle.

Understand the Rules

Firstly, it's all about researching and understanding the rules.

- Understand what your audience is talking about
- Listen to those conversations
- Find out what's uppermost in their minds

Secondly, engage with that audience using tools like Twitter (especially the search function to find relevant communities).

For example, you are a company that's responsible for producing software; it is easy to go out there and join in conversations with people who are journalists, or software providers themselves, or analysts, rather than just project your concept.

It's all about listening to those conversations; think of it like going to a party and arriving and finding out what everybody is already discussing. You wouldn't normally run up to a group of people and start shouting about the things in which you are interested.

- You would employ your social skills
- You would listen to what they're talking about
- You would contribute, listen, and acknowledge
- Then, you could find a way to put your own point of view across to a receptive audience

Form Ideas

Having done your research and started to form the ideas, think about how you are going to produce your content. First of all, you need to think about what kind of topic and what format. Will employees of your company be advocates for the content? Will it be a podcast or a video or a blog? Then, finally, think about the channels where you will distribute that content.

Create Content

At this point, you can produce content, and that's where small businesses often find a challenge. They imagine that creating content will be like writing an essay or an exam, with a blank piece of paper and the question at the top, which is: What do you want to write about today?

PETER SPRINGETT'S TOP TIPS FOR CREATING CONTENT QUICKLY:

- **Look for content that you already have**. It may be in the form of a brochure or an email, where you have explained something to a client or colleague. List out the key points and a list of bullet points, and conclude it with a call to action, and you will have the basis for a helpful blog

- **Use the Dictaphone on your phone**. Record your ideas as a conversation. Get the recording transcribed, or if you don't find it easy to have conversations with yourself, then find a colleague and ask them to ask you questions and record it

- **Use photos for inspiration** when you get stuck

- **You don't have to write a lot**. Remember that content doesn't have to be a 500-word blog. It could be a video or podcast that you have created with a couple of lines of scene setting

- **Curate content**. For example, saving links with shortcuts to a topic; over the week, you can quickly build up a great collection of stories. You can identify trends and use them to trace the story on a blog so that your audience can see what is hot and important to you

- **Posting a Tweet or LinkedIn update can be just as effective**. Work through your media feeds and look for interesting stories, and also curate stories that are relevant to your audience

- **Always carry a notebook**. Or have a notebook on your mobile device so that you can capture the idea when you have it. You can also record ideas onto your smartphone voice recorder

- **Sit down and have a conversation with somebody else**. Share their ideas and, again, record it or make notes, and you will find that bouncing ideas off a friend or a colleague is effective too

- **Don't expect to sit down at your desk and to come up with a great idea.** Peter finds that most of his ideas for any kind of work-related content start on a Saturday morning when he reads the newspapers and relaxes
- **Find a place** where you know those ideas will come out when you relax. You may find that it is a busy public space like a café or when you're out walking and exercising
- **Use a tool to collect your ideas.** Peter recommends Evernote and Pocket. So, when inspiration strikes while you are reading, you can save those links or stories.

PLANNING CONTENT

I asked Peter for tips about planning content:

He suggested creating a spreadsheet calendar with three different streams.

The first one is a business stream: It describes the journey of your business throughout the year.

The second stream is personal: What is your schedule for the next 12 months? This crosses into every aspect of your life at work, in the office, and at home. All these experiences have the potential to become the stories that bring your business to life.

The third stream is about your industry. For example, if you are selling wetsuits for triathlons, and the triathlon season is in the summer, from May until September, you know that most of your business will take place then. You may also know that in the first six months of the year, people start training to compete in those events, and it will probably be a little quiet afterwards, but then you may know that this is when trade shows take place.

So, take these things into account when you're planning.

'Consider how you make sure the content is appropriate for the time of year, and what will add value to that audience. It might inspire you to create content at that time in the training season, for example.

'What you are looking for are intersections in these three layers. For example, where people are talking about your customers at an industry event. You can then generate related content, using the event hashtag, which will appeal to the event audience as well.'

PETER'S TIPS FOR TOOLS TO PLAN

It doesn't have to be complicated. Most people will be familiar with a simple tool such as a spreadsheet. You can also use an online calendar such as Google Calendar, which works well.

Peter uses a project management application called Trello. Trello is a neat way of organising information and keeping track of content; for example, when it will be published, and the stage reached in the production cycle. It can also be used by content teams. www.trello.com

Thank you, Peter.

Creating Content that Matters to Your Customer

When you create content, you have to start with your customer in mind. What is in it for them?

It is worth imagining where your customer is in their buying cycle:

- Are they even aware that they need your product or services yet?
- Have they become aware that they have a problem, but maybe they are not yet aware of how to solve it?
- Are they looking for a solution to their problem?
- Are they looking at options?
- Do they need reassurance that your solution is the best possible solution for them?
- Do they need the details for how your product or services work?

Can you see that you can create content specifically for each of these stages? Approaching content creating in a systematic way will get you better results than randomly sitting down and writing what you feel like writing about. Think about the question that your customer may be asking on Google and write content or create a video to answer that question.

These days, most sales start online with a Google search. And a good part of the buying decision remains online, whether people research online or ask their social network for advice. Research shows that 70% or more of the buying decisions take place before the customer speaks to the company. The content you create should help them along the buying process by answering the questions they have at the time. More and more, buyers are looking to do their online research before they make a decision, and they often want to have detailed information about your products and how they work before they even pick up the phone to speak to you. Frequently, they want to see a demonstration of your product or understand how your services work so that they can make decisions before getting in touch with you.

Do you spend a lot of time answering the same questions over and over on phone calls; you know, the type of questions that you hear yourself going on autopilot to answer? There is a good chance that this information would be perfect for content for your website, blog, and Social Media. Think about how much time it would save if people contacted you when they are ready to buy from you.

Case Study—How a Piece of Content can Generate

New Leads for Years

EXPERT: ANDY FOOTE

Andy Foote teaches people advanced LinkedIn strategies and helps professionals build their personal branding on LinkedIn. At the beginning of 2013, he wrote a blog post called '*3 Stunningly Good LinkedIn Profile Summaries*'.

http://www.linkedinsights.com/3-stunningly-good-linkedin-profile-summaries/

It wasn't the first blog he's written or the last, but this post struck a chord and got talked about on top industry media sites. Shared widely, it has over 200 comments to date, and ranks as the top Google search for 'LinkedIn Summary'. Each month, this one blog post attracts over 45,000 people to his website. This traffic generates 10 – 15 new leads into his consulting business each week. Because the blog post is on topic, the enquiries he receives come from professionals who want to work with him. His LinkedIn profile ranked as the top most viewed profile out of 99 LinkedIn Experts/Coaches/Trainers on LinkedIn in 2015. I am a little jealous, of course!

> *Although it is unlikely that you will reproduce this amount of traffic from a single blog post, what you can learn from this is:*
>
> *Write content that would interest your ideal customers*
>
> *Create content with your clients firmly in mind*

Four Ideas for Creating Your Content Quickly

#1. Crowdsource Content using LinkedIn Groups and Twitter

Crowdsourcing content using LinkedIn Groups and/or Twitter offers several benefits:

1. It's quick because you are curating other people's words

2. By letting everyone who has contributed to your article know that it is live, most contributors will read it and share it with their community

TIPS FOR USING LINKEDIN GROUPS AND TWITTER TO CROWDSOURCE:

- Ask the Right question
- Consider asking the same question in other LinkedIn Groups, or more than once on Twitter
- People within a LinkedIn Group will give you a thoughtful, longer answer
- People on Twitter will give you a succinct quote that you can embed directly into your blog
- Make sure you follow everyone who helps you on Twitter
- Take the comments and write a blog post or publish directly on LinkedIn Published, making sure you give the correct source for all the quotes
- Send a message to each person that you have quoted in the blog to let them know. It is irresistible to people, and they will click through and share the content
- If they are not 1st connections yet, it is a good reason to ask people if they are happy to connect, whether they contributed via LinkedIn or Twitter

- Share the link to the post within the discussion thread
- Share the post as an update and tag the relevant people if they are 1st connections
- Share the link to people individually that you think would be interested, such as people in the same industry as the original group
- Tweet the blog post individually to let people know that it is live
- Tweet the blog post, thanking a few contributors each time you share it

---

#2. Use Existing Presentations for SlideShare

WHAT IS SLIDESHARE?

Think of SlideShare as the YouTube for presentations but with a strong business orientation. LinkedIn owns it, but SlideShare is also a content-sharing platform in its own right.

WHY SLIDESHARE?

- Easy to create content. All you need is Powerpoint or similar software. Upload your presentation onto SlideShare. Your presentation can be viewed and shared easily
- It's great for search. The title of the presentations on SlideShare appears high in Google searches. When you load a presentation onto SlideShare, it adds all the words on the slides as script, which is also indexed for search. People search within SlideShare for business content as well as via search engines
- Easy to share. It is simple to share the presentation onto your LinkedIn Profile or as an update, on Facebook and Twitter, and you can embed it within your blog too. People can flick through your presentation easily. People who view your presentation can share it across their networks with ease

- Lots of Eyes. SlideShare has over 70 million unique visitors each month, and most marketers ignore it. This means SlideShare is a great opportunity for business owners to shine
- Extra options. The premium version allows you to add video and capture emails directly, so it may be worth investigating it as an option for lead generation if you have an automated marketing system

In 2012, I delivered a webinar on how to Twitter for PR for Toastmasters Clubs. Due to a few technical issues, the slides weren't visible in the recording, so I posted my presentation onto SlideShare so that people could view the slides while listening to the recording. I didn't think much more about it.

About six months later, I had a notification from SlideShare congratulating me on achieving over a thousand views. Wow, that's a lot of eyeballs.

I looked at my profile. Oops, I hadn't even bothered to fill it in properly and hadn't included my website. What a lot of missed opportunities to connect. I looked at my slides. Without hearing my presentation, my slides wouldn't make much sense. Oops again.

It got me thinking. If over a thousand people had clicked on my slides without me promoting, and without me thinking of it as a standalone showcase, what would happen if I produced a presentation especially for SlideShare?

So, I re-purposed a popular blog post, 55 Things to Tweet About, and created a Powerpoint especially for SlideShare. I called it 'Tons of Things to Tweet About on Twitter'.

This is what has happened:

I woke up in the morning with an email from SlideShare congratulating me, again. They had chosen my presentation out of thousands uploaded the day before to feature on the Home Page of SlideShare. (I hadn't even realised that they had a Home Page.)

While I slept, 200 people had viewed it. I had gained more subscribers to my mailing list. During the first 24 hours, it became the most talked about SlideShare on Facebook, and Facebook included it in the 'Hot on Facebook' section of their Home Page. Within the first 48 hours, it had over 2000 views. Within that time, I had more LinkedIn connection requests and followers on Twitter than I had ever had before.

The presentation has had over 18,000 views to date and been embedded 800 times.

I can't guarantee that your presentation will have the same number of views, but all you need is the right customer to view your presentation. Worth thinking about.

TIPS FOR SLIDESHARE PRESENTATIONS

- Make sure that your presentation is branded with your business logo at the beginning and end
- Make sure that it is easy for people to get hold of you if they see your presentation in isolation. Does it include your website and contact information?
- Ensure your presentation makes sense if someone views it in isolation
- If you have images or presentations you can use already, it is straightforward to create a new presentation. Far faster than creating a video
- Think of the words you use in your presentation. SlideShare will transcribe these automatically and search index them. Have you used your keywords in your presentation?
- Once you've created a presentation, remember to share it on your LinkedIn Profile as well as an update and on Twitter and anywhere else you are connected

#3 Create Images for using on Social Media Quickly

WHY YOU NEED IMAGES

- It's quicker to produce an image than writing a blog
- Our eyes are naturally drawn to pictures, and a picture has more visual impact than text. Pictures also give you more display space or surface area on Social Media posts
- Our brains process visual images 64,000 times faster than text
- Approximately 65% of the population are visual learners
- A 2011 study by Skyward, showed that including images in your content leads to significantly more views. In fact, visual content receives 94% more views than content without an image
- Tweets with images get substantially more clicks, likes, and retweets than those without images. Every piece of research I've read shows this
- Pictures posted on LinkedIn do well too but make sure that they are business related

HOW TO GET IMAGES TO USE LEGALLY

In an ideal world, we would have tons of images created by designers ready and waiting for us to use. In the real world, few of the businesses I've worked with have a large stock of images. If you work with a designer, it's worth getting them to create templates for you to use so that your images are consistently branded.

I am always horrified by how many people think it is okay to use an image that they found on Google search. You are breaking copyright laws when you use other people's photos or images without their permission. Just because something is on the internet, doesn't make it all right for you to use. How would your business cope if you received a hefty fine for each image? It is happening more frequently than you think.

So, what are your options?

- **Pay for stock images**. You know you have the right to use, but if you choose popular images, you may see other people using them, and using a model in your image makes things look fake
- **Pay a photographer**. This professional can take photographs for you. Remember that the photographer owns the copyright of the photos, and that you need to make sure that the terms of use of the images include Social Media
- **Use photos for free** under creative commons licence. Personally, the small print left my head spinning, but if you are willing to look at the legalese, Flickr has plenty of great photos under Creative Commons
- **Take photographs yourself**. The quality of the cameras on smartphones has improved dramatically. People also love to see behind the scenes. Great apps exist that can help you to improve your images. Photographs taken on your smartphone are easy to add text to, using apps like WordSwag and incredibly easy to share to Social Media sites
- **Find great sources of free photographs**. Lots of sources give you permission to use their images

My two top sources for high-quality images:

Subscribe to Death to the Stock Photo and get sent monthly photos http://deathtothestockphoto.com/

Subscribe to Unsplash https://unsplash.com/ and you get sent ten photos every ten days

Get a more professional look with Canva

If you are on a tight budget and want to do the design work, I highly recommend that you look at Canva. It is an online graphic design platform that offers free access to a wide assortment of design tools and options. It saves you the hassle of working out dimensions for different platforms, and you can use it to create your LinkedIn Background and Twitter Header.

It is easy to get started, and they have a free 'Design School' to help you. The basic platform is free if you use your pictures, but they also have a good range of photos that you can buy for $1 each. They also have a premium option, but play with the free option first.

https://www.canva.com/

OUTSOURCE

- **Fiverr**.—Get someone else to create Social Media Images for you for $5 (about £3.50)
- **Upwork**.—Freelancers with all sorts of skills. The price varies from freelancer to freelancer
- **Virtual Assistants**.—Make sure that the virtual assistant has the skill set you're looking for
- **Designers**.—Most designers will create a series of templates for you to use with your corporate branding

#4 Use LinkedIn Publisher to Show Thought Leadership—

(Even if You Don't Have a Website)

LinkedIn Publisher is a great way to get your content in front of more people. Even if you have a blog, it is worth creating content especially for LinkedIn. LinkedIn Publisher allows you to create longer-lasting content. It is accessible to everyone with a LinkedIn account, and all your published content is visible on your profile. There is a good chance that if someone views your profile, then that someone will read some of the content you've written because LinkedIn places it right at the top of your profile.

It is straightforward to publish a post, and LinkedIn guides you through the process. Once you publish it, all your connections get a notification that you have a new post. Sadly, I see too many small businesses treat this as free advertising, a sales pitch, or a press release. Or, worse still, I see badly written pieces full of mistakes. Get someone to read over your article before you hit publish, or use Grammarly.

Hot Tip: Grammarly is a browser extension that checks your grammar and spelling for you. I highly recommend you look into installing it on your computer. It helps you write mistake-free in Gmail, Facebook, WordPress, Twitter, LinkedIn, and anywhere else you write on the Web. Simply hover over any word with an underscore to correct a mistake.

TOP TIPS FOR LINKEDIN PUBLISHED POSTS

- **Your headline attracts attention**, and there is no point in spending hours crafting a masterpiece if you add a headline as an after-thought. If your headline doesn't capture your audience's attention, your hard work will go unread

- **Always add a Banner Image** to your story. It doesn't have to be complicated. You can use a nice photograph or create an image using your branding colours and words. Canva is useful for creating images. You can also create images quickly using Powerpoint or PicMonkey

- **Break up text** with pictures, headlines, and bullet points. A block of text puts off most people. People tend to scan content, so make sure that your key points stand out

- **Longer posts seem to get shared more**, probably because they are more likely to contain content worth sharing. A short post might get views, but unless you are incredibly good at expressing yourself in a succinct way, it may not get shared

- **Include a call to action**. A call to action doesn't have to be salesy; it may be as simple as asking people to leave a comment or letting people know how to get in touch with you

- **End with a short bio** about you, the author. I know, it is LinkedIn and people can click to see your profile at the start of the piece, but is worth reminding them about who you are. They may have seen your post on someone else's timeline and clicked through and not noticed you were the author. Give people a reason to get in contact with you

- **After you've published your post**, don't miss opportunities by not responding to each and every comment. Make sure you look to see who views and shares your post too

Curating Other People's Content

In an ideal world, we would all have great writing skills, be brilliant in videos, and have the time to create great content, but if you are like so many other business owners, you probably wish you had more hours in a day. Some small business owners work 70 hours a week. You may have the budget to get someone else to produce content for you, which is great, but not everyone has or feels they can justify the expense versus the results each piece delivers individually.

Okay, so what do you do then? Well, the good news is that there is so much great content produced every day that by simply sharing that content, you become a valuable resource for other people. Sounds good, doesn't it?

Now, before you worry about stealing other people's content and breaking copyright, I am not suggesting that you take other people's content and pretend it is yours. Or write an introduction paragraph and link to someone else's content. Or even use a tool like Paper.ly or Scoop.it to create a virtual newspaper from other people's content. When I talk about curating, I am talking about having a process for sourcing great content easily and sharing that content on your Social Media feed.

Generally, if someone has sharing buttons on their blog, they actually want you to share the content. As a blogger, I actively encourage people to share my content so that I get more readers visiting my website. There is no point spending hours writing content if nobody reads it. All business owners I speak to would like free traffic to their website. When someone shares my content, it makes me notice them. By sharing other people's content, you become more noticeable.

The value you add to the original content is by:

- Adding a comment that gives people a reason they should read, watch, or listen to it

- Being selective about what you share. Know what your customers are interested in and filter the content so that you become a trusted source of high-quality information. Make sure you read the content before you share
- Selecting certain content that you know would be interesting to certain people and share that content with them directly. This can be done either by tagging them or sending it to them privately via direct message

Starting from scratch

If you know nothing about an industry at all and need to find content to share, I would recommend that you do the following:

- Google a few keywords about the industry
- From there, you will find great sources of information about the industry
- Make a note of the sources
- Click on the website and look at the content
- If the content looks useful, add the link to a spreadsheet
- Follow them on Twitter and add them to a Twitter list, and if they have a LinkedIn Company Page, follow them
- Find the names of the people who wrote the articles. Find them on Twitter, and if they are producing useful content in their Twitter stream, follow them and add them to the list
- Look at the headlines of the articles. Do certain phrases stick out? Google these and see what comes up
- Within an hour, you should be able to find enough useful content to keep going for a few weeks and have a useful Twitter list of sources of content

Starting with experience

Most of you won't be starting from scratch. You will have a good idea of the trade magazines for your industry and good sources of information about industry news. Most of these will have a website and Social Media Accounts. Find their Twitter account, follow it, and add it to a Twitter List. Have a look at their other Social Media Accounts. You will also have an idea of thought leaders. Find out whether they have a Twitter account and follow their LinkedIn account.

Use Twitter Lists to source great content easily - Make lists of news sources, great blogs, and people who provide useful industry news and relevant content for your business. Skim the list each day to find good content to share. You can create up to 1000 Twitter lists with 5000 accounts on each list; however, I think that a list of over 200 people defeats the purpose of using them to filter conversations. Twitter lists can be imported onto dashboards like Hootsuite and Tweetdeck easily.

LinkedIn news feed & Pulse - You can follow influencers (without needing to connect with them) and companies that provide great content as well as connecting to your industry peers to make your LinkedIn News Feed an interesting read. This will, obviously, vary from industry to industry. LinkedIn Pulse is an online news aggregator within LinkedIn designed to share self-published content. LinkedIn Pulse can be tailored to each individual. You can also search for stories of interest by category, popularity, and based on who your influencers are. *You can install LinkedIn Pulse as a separate app to your Smartphone.*

LinkedIn posts via search - Did you know that you can search LinkedIn posts by keywords? Well, you do now. Add your keywords into the search bar, and then choose the posts option, which currently you will find to the left of the search bar. At the moment, it is an icon with three horizontal lines and a small downward arrow. When you click on the arrow, one of your options will be posts. If it has changed by the time you read this book, send me a quick message on LinkedIn or tweet me, and I'll find it for you. You can even narrow the search down further to find the most recent posts.

Using Facebook to curate content - If you use Facebook regularly, did you know that you can set up Interest Groups or Lists in Facebook to curate content from good news sources? Setting up a list based on interest is easy to do. It is useful if you already know people or Pages on Facebook that consistently provide useful information. Even if you don't want to set up your own Interest List, you can find plenty of great lists that other people have curated already.

Useful Tools to Look at for Sourcing Relevant Content

Buzzsumo—http://buzzsumo.com/ This tool is extremely useful at sourcing popular content for almost any topic. You type in what you are interested in, and it will show you the most shared content on that topic. Buzzsumo makes it easy to find out what content works in an industry and who the major influencers are. Definitely worth looking at.

Scredible—https://scredible.com/ One of my favourite sources of hot-off-the-press content when I'm using my smartphone. Scredible uses artificial intelligence to find the best sources of content for you. You start by entering the type of content you are interested in and a few sources of content for your industry. It will then provide you with content. It learns what you are interested in by what content you read, bookmark, or share, and provides you with more relevant content. You can choose to share content on Facebook, Twitter, and LinkedIn either immediately, or you can schedule for later in the day.

Klout—https://klout.com/ Klout is a way to measure social influence, but it also has a useful source of topic-specific content, which you can either post to Facebook or Twitter straight away or schedule to post later. Have a look in the explore section of Klout.

Steps for Content Curating

1. **Know your industry influencers and good sources of information**—Google keyword phrases that you would like to be known for, and tools for finding influencers

2. **Use a tool to make curating easier**—e.g., Buzzsumo and Scredible

3. **Curating best practices**—Create Twitter lists & Facebook Interest Lists, and follow influencers and good news sources on LinkedIn and Twitter

4. **Use a tool to make reading easier**—e.g., Hootsuite

5. **Read** the content

6. **Find ways to store great evergreen content to share later**. This could be as simple as creating a spreadsheet with relevant links, but you could also use an app like Evernote to store helpful content to share later. I find Pinterest useful to pin articles that I might want to refer to later

7. **Share the content**—this may sound obvious, but the purpose of curating is to share the content to build your personal brand. Space out your sharing. Buffer App is a good tool for doing this. Too many links shared too close together look spammy. Add value by adding a comment when you share it. Learn how to plan and schedule content to make your life easier

Planning and Scheduling to Make Your Life Easier

I'm willing to bet that you don't want to spend every minute of your working day on Social Media.

Before you become horrified that you have to spend hours and hours online to do all of the things mentioned, know this—it doesn't have to take that long.

To do this, you need to plan what type of content you want to put out, as well as when and how often. I don't believe in automating human interaction, but I do believe that you will find Social Media easier if you plan ahead and schedule content to go out consistently. When you do this, you will have more time to show up and have conversations with people and engage. So, it isn't about putting everything on autopilot and walking away, hoping it will work for you, but more of a case of scheduling great content so that it goes out consistently, especially when you are busy with paid work.

Make sure that you show up and interact with people on a daily basis. It doesn't have to take more than fifteen minutes a day to check interactions on Social Media and respond to people if you are tight for time. The benefit of using your smartphone is that you can do this while you are waiting for meetings to start, waiting in a queue, sitting on a train, or even waiting for the kettle to boil.

Create a Simple Content Calendar

A content calendar doesn't have to be complicated. It can be as simple as using Flipchart-sized paper, writing on a whiteboard, creating spreadsheets, or using Google Calendar to plan what content you will post and when.

- Start by looking at the year ahead (or the next six months). Put in all your business events, marketing activities, and promotions
- Add in seasonal information that might be relevant for your industry
- Add in any big conferences, exhibitions, and shows
- Work out what type of content would be useful for your customer to hear. Remember, most of your content should be about helping your customers by providing relevant information to them, and not about doing press releases about your business

You may find it easy if you have set days for doing different types of content; for example:

Weekends: Support Local community events and show you are a member of your community

Monday: News about your business, special offers, or promotions

Tuesday: One type of tip

Wednesday: Behind the scenes and people news—any staff celebrations, birthdays, and you in action

Thursday: Another type of tip

Friday: Something fun/inspiring

- Is some of this information evergreen? Or, in other words, is there content that won't date? For example, if you were a laundry company, giving stain removal tips might be useful. It's helpful for your potential customers and relevant to your business, and stain removal tips will not go out of date. Another example of evergreen content would be if you were an accountant; every year, business owners will leave filling out tax returns until the last minute. The same reminders and advice could be used every year

- What content have you already created that could be used or repurposed easily? Do you already have information on your website that you could direct people to via Social Media? Do you have brochures with information that could be created as Social Media posts?

- Are there obvious pieces of content you need to create? Who will create the content? Can it be done internally, or will you need to outsource it?

- Are there great sources of information already published by other people that will be useful to share? Google is your friend. Source as many articles and videos around each different idea as you can within an hour. Save the heading and link onto a spreadsheet as you go

- If you want to publish hot-off-the-press news for your industry, look for people who constantly supply that information. Which media source provides consistent quality content?

- Decide which platforms you are going to be active on and how often you plan to post

Scheduling Content Tools

When you know what you want to post, where you want to post it, and how often you want to post it, it's time to get organised with a few tools.

Tweriod - This is a good little tool to use at least once to see which time your followers are on Twitter, and then you can see what the best time is to Tweet. If you only plan to schedule a few tweets a day, have a look at Tweroid to find out when your followers are active. You will get more response if you Tweet when more of your followers are Tweeting. The free version is limited but gives you an indication of when to schedule.

Hootsuite - Hootsuite is a Social Media Management Tool. It presents your Social Media channels as a dashboard. This makes it easy to keep track, monitor what other people are saying, and manage your Social Media channels. You can schedule content to go out across Facebook, LinkedIn, Twitter, Google Plus, and Instagram. It is worth paying for a premium account (at the moment it is under a tenner a month) because it allows you to bulk schedule up to 350 messages a month. Definitely more time effective than doing each one individually. I tend to use Hootsuite to schedule Tweets when I am speaking at events or have training or other events coming up so that it is done once and I don't have to remember to do it consistently.

Buffer - Buffer does a lot more than I tend to use it for and the premium is at a similar price to Hootsuite, so have a look at it too. Buffer allows you to add content into a buffer, which will then be shared at the optimum time across the day. I tend to use Buffer when I'm reading a lot of content and find many useful articles worth sharing. I don't want to fill my timeline with lots of links, so by loading them up to Buffer, I can pace out the links. It works across Twitter, LinkedIn, GooglePlus, and Facebook.

Tweetjukebox - I love this relatively new tool. At the moment, it only works for Twitter, but Tweetjukebox will become Socialjukebox soon, which offers options to schedule to other Social Media platforms. It is incredibly useful if you have evergreen content such as quick tips or 'how to' blog posts. You can put a certain number of Tweets out. I have pictures connected with those Tweets, and it will randomly choose which one to Tweet. I have Tweets going out from seven in the morning until ten at night at different intervals each day, and they will choose the Tweet for me. I have quite a few Twitter tips on Tweetjukebox and, since doing that, I have had more engagement and response. So, if I am busy, I know that some content is going out each day, but I do go onto Twitter every day and interact with people.

Stop Press

Twitter have just launched a Dashboard that allows you to schedule Tweets. Go to https://dashboard.twitter.com/i/landing to get started. Once you have set it up. Go to the 'Create' tab to schedule Tweets.

Time Management Tips for Content

- Monthly.—Plan your Content
- Monthly.—Make sure your content is scheduled
- Set notifications.—This way you can interact quickly
- Daily.—Interact with people
- Daily.—When you come across great content, do one of three things: Share, save, or schedule it
  - o Share it immediately with your network
  - o Save it for later, using a tool like Evernote or email yourself the URL
  - o Schedule it to post later, using browser apps like Buffer or Hootlet (by Hootsuite) or, if you have sourced the content within Scredible or Klout, use their built-in scheduling tools
- At least weekly.—Share targeted people's content

Inspiration for Everyday Posts on Social Media

Become a storyteller, talk about your brand, and tell a story.

For example, if you are writing a book at the moment, start by talking about the process of writing before you get ready to launch it or before you publish. Tell people some of the thoughts behind the chapters. Take pictures of the books and as the proofs are taken. All of that makes people connect, and then they become associated with it and involved.

If you are launching a new product or service, talk about working on something exciting well before you start official promotion of the launch.

Images are incredibly powerful. Make sure that at least some of your content is in picture form. Pictures give far bigger display space than a text-based post. I have noticed the difference it has made to my reach on both LinkedIn and Twitter. When I post a picture, I also get more interaction.

Keep your posts on LinkedIn business related. There has been a more recent tendency by some people to post more personal content like baby photos. Please, don't. LinkedIn is not Facebook, and I suggest you keep your business hat firmly on.

You don't have to post as often on LinkedIn as on Twitter.

If you never post any updates on LinkedIn, start by committing to posting once a week. Schedule it in your diary. If you already post occasionally, commit to three times a week consistently. If you post more frequently, try updating every day. If your content is interesting to other people, they will notice you for the right reasons.

Inspiration for LinkedIn

Here are a few ideas for what to post on LinkedIn as updates:

1. Industry news and trends
2. Statistics, reports, and research results for your industry
3. Your LinkedIn published posts (even if you wrote them a while ago)
4. Your company news and LinkedIn Company Page posts. They will get more visibility shared on your profile
5. Your opinions about content you share
6. Interact with other people's posts—it will be shown to your network in their feed
7. Tips and how to articles
8. Videos
9. Presentations. Put them onto SlideShare and share them on your Profile as updates
10. Content that you know your clients would be interested in, even if it is not directly about your industry

Inspiration for Twitter

Twitter needs a higher frequency of posting. If you only rarely Tweet, try posting once a day. When I started on Twitter, I decided that, come rain or shine, I would Tweet at least once a day. At the start, it felt difficult to think of something to say, but I've managed to Tweet more than 36,000 times now, and it stopped being a chore a long time ago. I suspect that a large chunk of those Tweets are conversations with other people. Every now and then, you will need a bit of inspiration for what to put on Twitter, and so here are a few ideas of what to say:

#1 Tweet any one of the following:

- Announce something
- Teach something
- Give relevant information
- Motivate someone
- Entertain someone
- Ask a question
- Answer a question
- Say something that is location specific
- Talk about your industry
- Talk about your profession
- Say what you are working on right; ask what they are doing
- Talk about what you are about to do
- Wish everyone a good morning/evening/weekend; preferably with a photo you've taken
- Tweet about something specific that is in the news
- Look at the calendar for something topical happening today
- Find the hashtag for an event you're going to attend and find people using the hashtag, follow them, and talk about the event
- Ask for help
- Crowdsource a blog post by asking people to help you
- Use a Twitter gif to show how you feel about something
- Use a Twitter poll to do some market research

#2 Random acts of kindness:

- Introduce someone to another person
- Give a positive review (remember to use the business or person's Twitter name)
- Make someone smile
- Congratulate someone for something you see in your feed
- Thank someone
- Tweet me to say that you are enjoying this book

#3 Start a conversation with someone on one of your lists:

- Ask them how their week is going so far
- Ask them if they are going to a particular event that you are attending if you are both in the same industry
- Find something they have been Tweeting about and respond to their Tweet
- Ask them what they think about a particular relevant article (sharing the link)
- Thank them for something they have done
- Join a conversation by replying to two people chatting
- Ask them for their recommendation for a restaurant/ software package/ tradesman
- Ask their opinion about something
- Wish them a happy weekend/lovely day
- Ask them for a top tip for a post you are writing
- Ask them which Twitter chats they would recommend

#4 Join a Twitter chat using a hashtag:

- There are so many Twitter Chats going on that it is likely that you will be able to find one any day
- Retweet interesting Tweets
- Answer the Question(s) of the day (QOTD) using the hashtag
- Use Quote Retweet to respond to conversations remembering to use the hashtag so that your Tweet is found
- Reply individually to anyone who mentions you, remembering to add the hashtag
- Follow people who interacted with you during the chat

#5 Share content:

- Share an old blog post with a question
- Share an old blog post with two relevant hashtags
- Share an old blog post with 'Please Retweet'
- Share an old blog post with an image

- Share a blog that someone on your lists wrote; make sure that you @mention their name
- Retweet an influencer's Tweet
- Retweet using the Quote Retweet to add your comment to someone on your lists post
- Retweet someone's Tweet using RT then their original Tweet
- Share an article about your industry using a hashtag
- Share an article about a subject that you know will be interesting and tag two people
- Share an inspirational quote

#6 *Trending topics:*

- Is there a relevant topic that is trending where you use the hashtag? CAUTION: Be sure you know what a hashtag is about before you use it.
- Is there a trending topic that you can Tweet your viewpoint about?

#7 *Share an image:*

- Share a snapshot of what you are doing or seeing right now
- Share a business book that you are reading at the moment
- Share a behind-the-scenes shot
- Share a group shot and tag everyone who is in the picture (you can tag up to nine people without it using your character space)
- Share up to four images in a Tweet to illustrate your product or services
- Share a motivational quote on an image
- Do a 'Thank you' image and thank people for something in particular
- Share an image that shows you are a human being
- Share an image that shows something that people in your area will recognise
- Share a selfie at a business event

- Share a selfie of your meeting (obviously with permission from everyone)
- Share a selfie of you with your audience when you speak
- Share a business quote on an image
- Set up Twitter cards so that your URL automatically Tweets with images

#8 Send a Direct Message:

- Send a DM to someone on your list that you have been Tweeting with for a while and ask them for a quick chat/ Skype/ coffee to get to know each other better
- Send a DM to someone that you would like to work with
- Start a Group DM about a particular business-related topic
- Send a DM to someone that you haven't spoken to for a while

#9 Share a video:

- Share a YouTube video
- Share a video via Vine or Periscope
- Use the video recording built into your Twitter app to share a short tip for your followers
- Use Twitter video recording to send a short message
- Personalise a video for a particular person

#10. Use one of the popular recurring hashtags for the day of the week

- Monday: #MCM (Man Crush Monday) or #MusicMonday
- Tuesday: #TravelTuesday or #TransformationTuesday
- Wednesday: #WCW (Women Crush Wednesday) or #HumpDay
- Thursday: #TBT (Throwback Thursday) or #ThankfulThursday
- Friday: #FBF (Flashback Friday) or #FF (FollowFriday)

Part 2 - Discover

It would be lovely if all you had to do was sit back and wait for customers to come to you, but in the real world, you will need to be more proactive about finding opportunities and potential clients. This section is about creating more opportunities to get business through active listening and searching.

CHAPTER 4

Discover through Social Media Listening

L istening is an under-developed skill for most people in everyday life. And when it comes to Social Listening, most people hardly make any effort at all. Many business owners use Social Media only to broadcast their message. They broadcast out sales messages on autopilot, and then they turn around and say that Social Media doesn't work for business. Their excuse for not listening? They're not interested in what people are eating for lunch! And they don't have time for inane chatter. They don't realise that conversation is good for business. Good conversationalists tend to be good listeners. Learning how to listen online, gives you a great advantage over your competitors.

So, what do I mean by listening?

When I talk about Social Listening, I mean more than just monitoring online conversations.

Social Media monitoring is a useful way to find out what is being said on the Internet. If you have a big budget, useful software exists that helps to make your monitoring easier, but the costs are often out of reach for most small business owners' pockets. With a bit of know-how, and the helpful tools available, you can set up listening dashboards yourself. There are also ways to search for real-time conversations that talk about the products or services you offer.

However, I want to talk about listening in more of an old-fashioned human-to-human kind of way. The human element of Social Media is often under-estimated. There is a reason for the word 'Social' in Social Media and Social Selling. People do business with people they know, like, and trust. Technology has changed dramatically, but human nature hasn't. Feeling seen, heard, and acknowledged are important to us, so why wouldn't they be important to our customers?

How do you think people would react to you if you wandered around the streets talking to yourself? Imagine how many friends you would have if all you ever spoke about was yourself and you never asked questions or listened. The normal rules of engagement apply online.

Why Social Listening is Important

SIX REASONS TO LISTEN

#1. To engage and build relationships - A good way to think of Social Networks is in terms of physical places you would go to meet people in real life. So, for example, Facebook could be a big party at someone's house, Twitter could be a cocktail party, and LinkedIn could be a business conference. All of these are good places to meet all sorts of people and make connections. Imagine if you barged up to everyone, handed out your business card, and delivered a sales pitch at them? I suspect that you would find people moving rapidly away from you and trying to avoid you. When you listen first to what people are saying, and talk about what they want to talk about, you build up better relationships.

#2. To hear what people are saying about you - The good, the bad, and the ugly. People are talking about you, hopefully. If nobody is, do they know your business exists? So many business owners think that if they go on Twitter, it will open the floodgates of negative comments. But guess what? People will have discussions about your business whether you are there to hear them or not.

If you are a nice person and good at what you do, most people will be saying nice things about you, your service, or your company. It is great to hear compliments. Imagine if you were to write a lovely letter of praise to a company, and they don't even acknowledge your letter. How would you feel? Would you do it again? If there is a problem or a complaint, it is better to know about it.

If there is a problem or a complaint, it means you can handle it properly. By responding to comments, queries, and complaints in a helpful and professional way, your customers are more likely to buy from you again.

#3. For competitor analysis - Have you thought about what you can learn by monitoring not only what your competitors are posting about, but also what their customers are saying? Here are a few things that might be useful to look at:

- Press coverage they're getting: Not only good for finding out what they are up to. It is also great for sourcing media that publishes content about your industry, and journalists that write about your niche. If they have covered your competitor, they will probably be open to writing about your story
- News: Are there opportunities or market trends you need to be thinking about?
- Content Marketing Strategy: What type of content do they post? How is it working for them? Are they getting much engagement and shares? What would you do the same? And what would you do differently?
- Customer Feedback: Is there a gap that you could fill?
- Customer Complaints: Potential leads for your business if handled well
- Learning: What are they doing well that you could adapt?

- Avoiding: What are they doing badly?

#4. To learn news about your industry and local area - There is so much information out there. Following thought-leaders and influential people in your industry is a quick way to bring an endless source of relevant content direct to your news stream. You can't read everything, of course, but you can gain so much knowledge.

#5. To find out if people have expressed a need for your product or services - People are constantly talking and asking for advice online, in real time. If you sell widgets, and someone is asking for advice about widgets, you would be a fool not to listen. Discussions are going on all the time within groups on LinkedIn, Facebook, and Google+, and directly on Twitter. Searching for phrases that your customers might be using to ask for your product or service is a great way to reach potential customers. People are far more likely to recommend you if you are active on that platform, and they can tag you, than if they have to email you separately about it.

#6. To Smile, be Amused, and Inspired - When you listen on Social Media, there is an added benefit: You'll find that you enjoy Social Media more. There's so much humour online and so many lovely stories that I would be incredibly surprised if you couldn't find one thing to make you smile every day. You'll feel part of a community, and online strangers will become friends.

Be honest: How much time do you spend listening online?

SOCIAL LISTENING TIPS

I couldn't write about listening without mentioning Dale Carnegie. Even though he wrote his book decades ago, it is still relevant today.

> 'So, if you aspire to be a good conversationalist, be an attentive listener. To be interesting, be interested. Ask questions that other persons will enjoy answering. Encourage them to talk about themselves and their accomplishments. Remember that the people you are talking to are a hundred times more interested in themselves and their wants and problems than they are in you and your problems. A person's toothache means more to that person than a famine in China, which kills a million people. [...] Think of that the next time you start a conversation.'

Dale Carnegie on 'How to Win Friends and Influence People'.

People are having conversations online all the time. They may even be talking about you. Do you know if they are and what they are saying about you? Relevant conversations for your business take place within Facebook and LinkedIn Groups, but the best place for listening to conversations in real time is on Twitter.

Do you know?

- What your Customers are talking about
- Who influences your buyers
- What questions they are asking
- What your competitors are doing
- Whether there are early buying signals and what they are

Listening is where Twitter shows its true strength. Online conversations are easy to search for and follow in real time. All Tweets are now Google-Indexed.

Practical: How to Listen on Social Media

The problem is that you simply will not have time to listen to every single conversation on Twitter. Over half a billion Tweets go out every day. It's also unlikely that you will have the resources to listen to conversations twenty-four hours a day, seven days a week. So, here are some tips to keep you aware of what's going on without costing you a penny or losing your sanity:

1. Create Alerts so that you get email notifications
2. Learn to filter conversations so that you are not overwhelmed
3. Create a listening dashboard to make life simpler

How to Create Alerts

How do you find out what people are saying about you when you are not there? If someone is mentioning you or your business online, don't you want to know about it so that you can react? In most cases, this will be to thank them for saying something nice, but you will also want to know if someone has something negative to say about you. A business will typically hear from only 4% of its dissatisfied customers; 91% of unhappy customers will go elsewhere. (Source: 'Understanding Customers' by Ruby Newell-Legner.)

Customers whose complaints are resolved will go on to be more loyal customers than they were before.

It is useful every once in a while to do a search for your business on Google or Yahoo to see what you can find. Use an Incognito search for Google so that your results aren't personalised for you. There are three tools that I've found good for picking up mentions of your business online and sending you an email. If your search requirements are simple, you can get away with using the free versions. I would recommend that you try all three of these tools.

Google alerts https://www.google.co.uk/alerts Useful for picking up mentions in articles and blog posts. It only tends to pick up top search results, which means a lot of mentions will not get picked up.

Mention alerts https://mention.com/en/ I highly recommend this tool because it tends to pick up far more content than Google Alerts and not just in blogs or news stories. This tool is great for finding Social Media mentions across Facebook, Twitter, YouTube, and Google Plus. They allow one free search term before you pay. Mention have a forever-free version, which all free trial users are switched to automatically after 14 days. The free plan includes one alert and 250 mentions per month and, whenever you invite another user to sign-up for a free trial, you will receive a permanent addition of 100 mentions. You can create a bundled alert that can monitor up to five competitors for a particular keyword.

Talkwalker alerts http://www.talkwalker.com/alerts Works in a similar way to Mention. You may find it useful to use in conjunction with Mention so that you get more search terms. Worth looking at their free trial offer for unlimited search over seven days, looking at 'Results, Influencers, and Trending Topics' within Twitter, Facebook, blogs, news, and data coverage.

Twitter notifications If you are not on Twitter most of the day, it is probably worth setting up notifications so that you get alerted each time someone mentions you on Twitter, using your Twitter name. This can come through to you via email or on your phone. Have a look in your Twitter settings. You can also be alerted to Direct Messages (DMs). If you want to stalk or, I should say, pay attention to certain people, you can get alerted each time they post.

How to Filter Conversations

The sheer quantity of content generated on Twitter alone is phenomenal. A billion Tweets every two days. It is impossible to listen to everything, let alone all the content that people you follow Tweet. So, how do you filter the noise so that you can hear without being deafened?

- Be selective to whom you pay attention to
- Be selective and choose relevant conversations

Two useful ways to filter the conversation are using Twitter lists and hashtags.

One of the most under-rated tools already built into Twitter is Twitter lists. I'm astonished how many people who have been on Twitter for years still haven't discovered their usefulness. Twitter lists are an important building tool for Social Selling.

Twitter Lists

The fundamentals that you need to know:

- You can create up to 1000 lists
- You are allowed to have up to 5000 Twitter accounts in each list, but I would recommend that you don't add more than 100 accounts to each one. The lists become too noisy, which defeats the purpose of having lists in the first place
- You can choose a short title for the list and add a description
- Lists can be Private or Public, and there are tactical reasons to use both

- When a list is public, people can see that they have been added to the list, they can also see the name of the list, the description, and who is on the list. They can choose to subscribe to the list

Creating a name for your list:

- It can't start with a hashtag
- It will be public by default, so either call it something obvious so that you know what it is, or something flattering so that the people who get added feel pleased
- If you want to make the list private, you will have to edit the list on Twitter.com
- List names can't be more than 25 characters (you can add more than 25 characters in IFTTT, but it will be cut off after 25 on Twitter, which looks bad. I've done it. Oops!)
- List names have to start with a letter
- You can have numbers in your list name, but not symbols like #

FIVE DIFFERENT WAYS TO USE TWITTER LISTS

#1. Sort out your followers in groups. - There are all sorts of reasons you might choose to follow someone. For social listening, it is important to quieten the noise so that you can focus on the people most important to you. And the way you do this is by putting them into groups so that you can pay more attention to them at different times. These lists can be imported into Hootsuite and Tweetdeck to create a Listening Dashboard, which we will be talking about next.

The choice of how you want to divide your Twitter World is completely up to you.

- It helps you to organise your followers so that you can listen more to the people that interest you the most
- You don't have to put everyone you follow onto a list
- Lists can be private, so you can monitor people (such as competitors) without them knowing

- If you are using Hootsuite or Tweetdeck, you can use your lists as your columns feed

#2. Name your Twitter lists strategically. When you add people to a Public list, they get a notification that they have been added, which has benefits because it gives them a gentle reminder that you exist. This is one of the tactics that will be covered in the Nurture section of the book.

- Attract attention by calling your lists something interesting or obvious
- Most people like being added to flattering sounding lists. It will get their attention, and they are more likely to click on your profile to find out more about you
- Most people don't add a description to a list, but this gives an opportunity to explain why they have been added
- I know someone who has gained business by adding a cheeky description, which meant potential customers engaged with her

#3. Put people on lists rather than following them. If you are interested in certain people, but you want to keep your stream uncluttered, you can follow people on lists rather than following them. This means that you can find out what people are tweeting about by looking at the lists rather than your main feed.

- The advantage of this is that you can minimise the noise in your stream
- You can monitor people without them being aware that you are paying attention if your list is private
- You can put people on a list who are attending an event or using a hashtag without having to follow them

#4. Follow other people's lists. Rather than spending time curating a list, you can follow other people's lists.

- If people have curated a list of people attending a conference, you can simply follow the list rather than having to recreate your own
- You can follow anyone's public lists by going to their profile, searching through their lists, and clicking on the 'Subscribe' button
- A great source for lists worth following is Listorious—a third-party site that maintains a categorised directory of Twitter lists
- These can be imported into a Hootsuite listening dashboard too

#5. Search other people's lists for interesting people to follow. If you are looking for interesting people to follow, it is worth looking at the lists of people you already follow. Twitter.com has more functionality than the mobile apps. I would suggest that you use your computer to follow people on a list. See whether they are using lists by clicking on their profile. It is an easy way to find relevant people.

- If you know someone through a mutual networking group, the list of people they know may include people you know too
- If you know someone is based in a certain location, a list of local tweeters that they have created is useful
- Many business accounts will have a list of employee's Twitter accounts
- Many people who work for a company will list co-workers
- People will often have lists of people in the same industry

I have found some brilliant people this way. We will talk more about finding people in the next section.

25 IDEAS FOR TWITTER LISTS

1. Private lists of competitors
2. Private list of customers
3. Private list of potential customers
4. Private list of your employees and business partners
5. Private list of a few people that you want to notice you
6. Public list called Influencer
7. List called Special People
8. List based on Twitter chat
9. List of journalists in your industry
10. List of Bloggers who blog about your industry
11. List of people attending an event including speakers
12. List around a shared interest
13. Great sources of industry news
14. Thought leaders
15. News sources
16. Great source of local news
17. People that you know consistently have great content around a specific area
18. People you would recommend to follow
19. People you know from networking group
20. People who retweet you a lot
21. Great resources that would appeal to your potential customers
22. Celebrities in your industry
23. Business Leaders
24. List based on Boolean search criteria—how to do this is covered in the Finding People Section
25. List curated automatically for you by @DoYouEvenList*

*Tip: Do You Even List curates a list of your top people that you engage with each week. https://www.doyouevenlist.co/

Hashtags

Hashtags are a hashtag symbol followed by a word or a stringofwordstogether. They are a way of grouping conversations. So, for example, if you are watching a TV programme, there is often a hashtag for it. By following the hashtag, you can see what people are saying about the show, and by adding the hashtag to your Tweet, you can join the conversation. Hashtags are a great way of filtering conversation quickly. If you know particular hashtags are being used for your industry, or for an event, you can follow all the conversations about it by simply clicking on the hashtag.

TOOLS THAT WILL HELP YOU FIND THE RIGHT HASHTAGS FOR YOU

Hashtags.org—This will help you to find what a hashtag is about

Ritetags—This will help you to find the right hashtags for you to use

Hashtagify.me—This will help you to find relevant hashtags based on keywords

There are more, but these are excellent.

Ninja Tip—Hashtags to know if you want to build relationships with journalists and get free publicity:

#JournoRequest—journalists and bloggers looking for people to interview for stories.

*#URGHARO—for urgent stories to **Help a Reporter Out***

How to Create a Listening Dashboard

HOW TO SET UP A LISTENING DASHBOARD FOR FREE

The easiest way to set one up is to use a Social Media Management Tool like Hootsuite or Tweetdeck. I'm Hootsuite Certified, so I'll go through how to do it on Hootsuite.

If you haven't done so already, set up your Hootsuite account and add your social networks. Hootsuite is free. The premium version is more useful for managing multiple accounts and scheduling, but you may want to test the waters with the free version.

Before we get to any of the technical stuff about Hootsuite, it's worth thinking about how you're going to use it to listen.

- Listen to conversations to find opportunities
- Listen to gain business intelligence about your industry
- Listen to particular people to build and nurture relationships
- Listen to hear what your customers are saying about you

The nice thing about using Hootsuite is that you can respond to Tweets when you see something interesting and can allocate tasks to other team members. Hootsuite even allows you to save standard responses as templates if your business gets asked the same questions over and over again.

Hootsuite has two layers: Tabs and Streams.

Tabs

Normally, you will create a tab for each of your social networks. You can monitor ten streams within each Tab. So, for example, my Twitter tab has the following streams:

HomeStream, mentions, messages, pending tweets, my Tweets, new followers, and a few streams based on Twitter lists and searches.

You can add streams to your Twitter tab, but you will find it more helpful to set up different tabs for different objectives such as competitors, conversations, or influencers. You can set up to fifty tabs with ten streams each.

Streams

When you add a stream to your Tab, you have a few different options:

You can choose which network to connect to. You can search any public Twitter or Google+ posts easily. Facebook and LinkedIn options will only search for conversations from your existing connections or friends.

If you connect to Twitter with your Twitter Profile, the Twitter option gives four choices: stream, search, keyword, lists.

- **Stream**—This gives you normal Twitter functions to add as streams
- **Search**—You can use Boolean search within this one

> **Hint:** *Easier still, they give you a little button called 'Show Examples'. This will show you how to search for particular queries. It makes a useful crib sheet. We will cover Boolean search in the next chapter.*
>
> **Hint:** *You also have a small arrow in the search box, and when you click on that, you can localise your search result for your location.*

- **Keyword**—You can choose up to three keywords or phrases.

    Personally, I find Search more useful because you can search for keywords within the Search section, but you might find the keyword section more user-friendly

- **Lists**—You can import any list that you or anyone else has created. Yes, anyone else. So, if someone else has created a list of delegates for an event, then all you have to do is import it into Hootsuite, and you can monitor it more closely

A quick word on the differences between a stream using a search term and Twitter list for that search term:

If you set up a stream on Hootsuite for a search term, for example, #Surreychat (which is a chat I take part in most Saturday mornings), your stream will show you only the tweets using that hashtag.

If you create a list based on the hashtag #Surreychat, it will add the people who use that hashtag, so the stream would show the tweets and retweets of people who take part in #Surreychat. Only on Saturday morning, during the chat, would it include the hashtag #Surreychat.

> *Tip: If you are not sure what keywords or search terms to use, Hootsuite has a Quick Search option. In the top right of your dashboard, you'll find Quick Search. You can look up terms or phrases that might work. When you find ones that work, click on the 'Save as Stream' button, and it will be added as a stream within your open tab. Simple.*

Practical Example of a Tab

I have a tab set up for Media. I have used different search queries, which we will cover in the next chapter. In this tab, I have the following streams:

- A Twitter List of Small Business Journalists (a list that I created)
- A Twitter List of Local Press and Journalists (a list that someone else created)
- A Search for two local radio stations called 'from:bbcsurrey OR from:eagleradio' (the query from:username collects tweets from

that Twitter account. I'm collecting the tweets from two accounts by using the Boolean term 'OR')

- A Search based on #Journorequest
- A Search based on #PRRequest OR #Bloggerrequest
- A Search to see all the Tweets from @helpareporter called 'from:helpareporter'
- A Search for #URGHARO

Somewhere on your dashboard, make sure you have a stream to monitor mentions of your company name. Not all your customers will use your Twitter account name when they are talking about you, so make sure you listen out for all your mentions; e.g., my name is my brand, and most people will use my Twitter name @NickyKriel. To make sure I capture all of these, I would use 'nickykriel' in case someone has used a hashtag with my name too. I would make sure that I also search for the phrase 'Nicky Kriel', and I might also include some misspellings of my name like 'Nicki Kriel' or 'Nikki Kriel' or 'Nicky Kreil', for example.

Search is not case specific, by the way.

Remember: No matter how many tabs and streams you set up, a listening dashboard is completely useless unless you use it to LISTEN!

Stop Press

Twitter have just launched a Dashboard (https://dashboard.twitter.com) which allows you to customise your settings in the 'About You' tab to make sure you don't miss important Tweets. This tab shows you all your mentions of your Twitter name and username. In addition, you can add nicknames, unique hashtags and members of your team

CHAPTER 5

Discover Potential Customers through Search

Both LinkedIn and Twitter are incredibly useful for finding new customers, influencers in your industry, suppliers, and potential business partners. LinkedIn tends to be slightly better at finding people if you know the job titles you are looking for or the type of companies you want to work with. Twitter is great for finding people talking about your product or services and who might need your services right now. Often, it is easy to find the right people you want to connect with on LinkedIn, start following and interacting with them on Twitter, and then connect with them on LinkedIn. People tend to be more approachable on Twitter, and you will get the best results if you use both. Sometimes, the best place to start might even be using Google search.

Stop Searching; Start Finding

Research your potential business partners, customers, and what they are looking for

When someone contacts you via your website or email, do you research a bit about them before you speak to them? LinkedIn is a great resource for researching people before you meet up with them. You may meet people at a networking meeting and arrange to meet for a coffee. It is easy to assume that you know about them because you met them face-to-face and you had a short chat, but imagine the difference it would make if, when you meet them, you show that you have done research. It will also give you questions to ask them. Things to look at are:

- Website(s).—If you met them in person, there is a strong chance that they gave you their business card, but if they haven't, their LinkedIn Profile is a good source
- Company Page
- Twitter Account.—Often, people will be more human on their Twitter Account; it is worth spending a few minutes to see what their bio says about them, and look at their last few Tweets. Follow them while you're doing this
- Past experience.—Have you worked for any similar companies, or do you know someone who works for one of their past companies? Usually, people won't think their past experiences are worth mentioning, especially if they work in a different business now, but they may have a wealth of experience
- Blog/LinkedIn Publisher.—What do they write about? Is there something nice you can say about what they have published?
- Recommendations.—What other people are saying about them. Who have they worked with in the past that might be of interest?
- Contacts.—Do you share mutual acquaintances that you could speak to directly? Do they have any contacts that look like they would be good for your business to know?

Search to find and connect with potential customers

- LinkedIn is probably the world's most useful database for a business. You have over 400 million business professionals' data at your fingertips, and it is free
- Learn how to use the advanced search function to find potential customers
- See how you are already connected to them

- Do they share a group with you? Do you know someone who could introduce you to them?
- Read their profile thoroughly
- Make contact

How to Find People on LinkedIn

Would you like to know how to find people that might be interested in your products and services? Are you using the search function on LinkedIn thoroughly?

> **Warning:**
>
> *Make sure your profile is filled in 100% and is up-to-date before you start contacting people.*
>
> *Spending hours researching people to contact, and then not taking action, is a waste of time.*
>
> *Do not spam people when you find them.*

Again, the normal rules of engagement apply in Social Media. Don't do things via Social Media that you wouldn't do in real life.

LinkedIn is also a database that lots of people seem to forget, and the amount of information that you can obtain from there is phenomenal. If you think about it: When you fill in your profile for LinkedIn, you complete it in a structured way—unlike other Social Media platforms, such as Twitter, where you just give an email address to sign up. On LinkedIn, you are asked for a lot of data, such as where you worked in the past and what years you worked there.

How to Search on LinkedIn

The search section doesn't look like much, does it? However, it does far more than just finding people by their name.

One of the most powerful things about LinkedIn is its search capability, and that is because people enter their information in such a methodical way.

This means that you can look for keywords in specific fields. For example, you could look for someone who uses a particular term or phrase in his or her current experience, or who works for a specific company. I would suggest that you use the advanced search straight away because it gives you so many more options.

You can search for keywords in many areas within LinkedIn. If you click the advanced search button on the right, it opens up a screen that shows you can be specific when searching connections. For example, you can find people within ten miles of your postcode if you are focusing on local business.

By refining the search further, you can get targeted. If you are a basic account holder, you can further define your search by:

- Industry
- Relationship (this means how you are connected on LinkedIn; i.e., 1st, 2nd, or 3rd connection or group member)
- Language
- School
- Past Company
- Location
- Non-profit and volunteering interest

You don't have to enter a keyword in the 'keyword' section. So, for example, if you are looking for Managers of Hotels, you might enter the word

'Manager' to the 'Title' field and choose the 'current' option and the word 'Hotel' to the 'Company' field and, again, choose the 'current' option.

LinkedIn is especially clever because it allows you to find out how you are connected to that person. If they are a second connection, it means that you share at least one mutual contact. Click on the 'shared connections' to see who you know in common.

> *Tip: You can save up to three searches on your basic account and will be notified by email if new people sign up who fit within your search criteria.*

Using Advanced Search for Research

How much research do you do using LinkedIn? I will now talk about something called Boolean Logic. Before your eyes glaze over, take a deep breath—there is a reason for me doing this.

- Computers and databases are based on Logic
- LinkedIn Search and other searches on the Internet use Logic to get results
- Understanding a tiny bit about Logic will help you get better search results
- If you understand how search works, you will understand how you can be found
- By learning how search for keywords works, you can get savvier about the keywords you use

There is no point being fabulous if nobody can find you.

BOOLEAN SEARCH IN A NUTSHELL

Boolean Logic refers to the logical relationship between search terms.

There are three main ones:

- AND
- OR
- AND NOT

Remember Venn Diagrams?

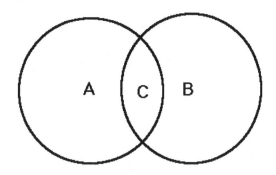

You have two groups of People:

Let's call one group A and the other group B. Some people will be a member of both groups, and those are called C.

Using a personal example, I have friends who are Toastmasters (A) and friends who are NLP Practitioners (B). Some of my friends are both Toastmasters and NLP Practitioners (C).

When you use 'AND' to search, you find the terms that are both. So 'AND' finds only the intersecting group (C).

When you use 'OR', you will get everyone who fits into either of the two groups. So, the term 'OR' will find everyone who fits into A and B groups.

In my example, it will be all my friends that are Toastmasters or NLP practitioners.

The term 'AND NOT' will exclude one group. So, if I wanted to find all my friends that are Toastmasters, but want to exclude all the people who are NLP Practitioners, I would get A without the C part.

One more useful search tool to know about:

'Quotation marks'

If you are looking for an exact term that people might use to describe what they do, put the term in quotation marks, and the search will look for that exact term. For example, if I am looking for business development consultants, I would use 'business development consultants', and then only the people using that exact term will be found.

Each box you complete in the Advanced Search creates an 'AND'. The search will look for results that match both criteria.

Within each box, you can use 'AND', 'OR', and 'AND NOT', and put terms in quotation marks.

Learning how to search properly will help you find customers or business partners.

Why cold call when you can connect with people directly on LinkedIn? There is a wealth of information on LinkedIn that can be incredibly useful to your business. Once you have done advanced search, don't forget to save your searches so that LinkedIn can email you when new people meet your criteria.

Ninja Tricks for Search

Something you need to realise about LinkedIn is that very few people will ever search for more than the basics. If you learn how to ask better questions, you will get better answers. Every word that anyone has entered on LinkedIn can be found if you really want to find it. If you are serious about finding people, it is worth paying for a premium version of LinkedIn, even if just for a month. You will get more search results.

LinkedIn's Top activity is searching for and finding people. And recruiters tend to be the top searchers. Tips that I've picked up from recruiters:

What can you do that other people are not doing?

If you only search with obvious keywords, you will only find the tip of the iceberg.

- People are human and often misspell words and use abbreviations
- Frequently, people who work in the industry won't mention any keywords, so it is always worth looking at a few profiles of people you know are your ideal customers and jotting down common words and phrases and including these in your search
- Most people will start with the top search results and only work their way down through the first page or two. If you start at the bottom, you will get different results from everyone else
- When you do a good search, make sure you work your way through all the people over a period of time; otherwise, you won't get the full benefits of the search results. Most people won't. Consistency pays dividends
- You can create long strings for search. Save them on a spreadsheet so that you can use them later
- Think about searching for verbs rather than nouns. Nouns are labels or job titles; verbs are what people do

- All fields can be used for Boolean logic
- Don't stop on the first search results

Techniques that will give you more advanced search results:

Create Long Searches (and save them on a Spreadsheet).

Do a search, including every word you think the people in that category might use. Separate the words with 'OR' to create a long OR string

Search by phrases and keywords that people in the industry use

Further refine a list of search results for particular phrases and keywords to improve results. Start with general words, and then look for words not mentioned.

- Do a search based on a keyword that you know is used in the industry
- Look for associated words that are in people's profiles
- Do a search including your original keyword and the associated words
- Then look for more associated words that are in profiles you find
- Do a search including these plus the other words
- Long string of OR 'phrase or keyword' OR 'phrase or keyword' OR 'phrase or keyword'

Implicit search

- Look for implied words. Search for a mixture of using keywords, job titles, and groups. Remember, you can exclude words strategically

Search using natural language

- Search on a few profiles that you know are good examples of your customers
- Search within their summary and job descriptions for the natural language they use and the phrases that crop up within all these profiles
- Do searches for these phrases or words
- Search for verbs that they use

Use Google Search to find people and groups

If you are not connected with someone as a first or second connection or in a Group, LinkedIn will hide the details about the connection. There is a way around this.

Go to Google

Type in: 'site:linkedin.com/in'

Plus whatever information you can see about the profile. For example, if it shows where they work or their title or professional headline, then add these in quotation marks. An example of this is if you wanted to finding people in a certain LinkedIn group, in this case 'CEO Success Network', you would use the Group name as a search term.

site:linkedin.com/in 'CEO Success Network'

Google will give you the first and last name of the person's public profile.

You can also use this trick to search within LinkedIn Groups if you are looking for people in that group who live in a particular location.

Other Useful Places to Look in for Potential Customers

- **Company Pages.**—Company Pages will show their employees and how they are connected to you. If you are interested in getting into a particular company, this is useful for knowing who to start building relationships with, either on LinkedIn (by connecting or joining the same group that they belong to) or off LinkedIn; for example, using Twitter as a way to connect. If you want to get into a company, you might think about using advanced search to see first or group connections that have worked for that company in the past. They may be able to give you valuable information

- **Alumni search.**—You might be surprised at what some of the people you went to university or school with are doing now. Never underestimate old connections

- **Your connections' network.**—Whom are they connected to that looks interesting?

- **Testimonials.**—Look at people who do similar things to you; have a look at the type of companies that are doing business with them by looking at who is giving them testimonials

- **Comments on industry related content.**—If you find a good post on LinkedIn Publisher, take the time to read through the comments section. Are there any people that look interesting to you?

- **Look at who's viewed your profile regularly.**—Often, people who are thinking of using your service will look at your profile, and even just looking at their profile may encourage them to send an invitation. Obviously, if you think they look interesting, you don't have to wait for them. Send them a personalised invitation, giving them a reason to connect

How to Use Groups to Find the Right People

How are you using Groups to connect to people on LinkedIn? LinkedIn allows you to join 100 groups. Groups allow you to build relationships online with members who may be influential in building your business. Reasons to join LinkedIn Groups:

Find new people who share your interests. You can communicate directly to members of the group even if you are not connected via message. LinkedIn has restricted the number of interactions you can have to 15 a month. You can follow group members if you are interested in what they say. If you engage with group members, you can ask them to connect with you. I choose the option 'Friend' because you don't need to have their email for this option. Always write a personal note, even if it is as simple as, 'We are in X group together, and I have enjoyed your answers to some of the discussions, and I would like to connect with you.'

Find influencers in your industry. Remember that you can learn from other people in your groups, and there will be always be people who are pleased to help you. Make sure you spend time reading relevant discussions in highly active groups. Add comments when someone you consider influential posts in the group.

Show your expertise in your field. LinkedIn Groups offer you a great opportunity to showcase your knowledge and expertise in your field by the way you answer questions and the discussions you start, as well as how you respond in general. Make sure you've joined groups relevant to your skills. Show that you are a thought leader by producing or curating good content that you feel happy to share with the group. Make sure you check the group's rules. Look at the profiles of everyone who interacts with you within the group.

Increase your network. Each group you join increases your network.

In search, 1st, 2nd, and groups show up first. It is worth joining at least one group with large numbers, as long as it's relevant, solely for the purpose of increasing your chances of being found. Join as many groups as you can, as long as they are relevant. Where is your customer likely to hang out?

Be strategic about how you use Groups. It would be impossible to be active in a hundred groups, but if you select a few targeted ones, you can improve your visibility. I would also recommend switching off the notifications for most of the groups once you have selected which ones you want to be active in; otherwise, you will feel as though you are being bombarded with emails.

You can select how often you want to be contacted—daily, weekly, or never. You can either do this by visiting the group or through your settings on your profile.

Join a few groups at a time that look interesting to you, and then spend a bit of time investigating each one before selecting which ones are worth focusing on.

- Choose 3 – 5 groups
- That have at least a few hundred people
- But no more than a few thousand
- In your target demographic
- Visit these groups at least once a week

It is more important to spend time where your potential customers are rather than your peers.

- Answer the most popular discussions
- Start discussions within the group to increase your visibility
- An email gets delivered to members of the group either daily or weekly, which shows them the top discussion too

- Look at Groups that your (potential) customers or people in your network have joined. You can find this section at the bottom of their Profile
- Set a goal to use the 15 intragroup messages you are allowed each month to speak to potential customers via groups

LinkedIn allows you to see your group activities at a glance. If you access groups via the Interests tab, it shows you the highlights from groups. You can change the order in which these appear in the settings (the cog symbol to the right) so that your favourite groups are displayed first. The Discover section is incredibly helpful for suggesting groups that you might be interested in. Worth checking.

Remember: Do not use groups to deliver sales pitches. You will get further if you are seen as someone who is a helpful part of the community rather than someone who is only there to promote themselves.

> *Tip: Each group has an individual set of rules. Some groups will flag you for sharing any link, while other groups encourage you to share your blogs. Make sure that you are aware of the group etiquette.*

How to Find Your Ideal Customers on Twitter

So, assuming that you know whom you want to target on Twitter, here are five ways to search on Twitter to find your ideal customers:

#1. SEARCH

It may sound obvious, but using the Search Function of Twitter is useful for finding people who are interesting to you.

A few things you need to know about search:

- It is not case sensitive
- You can search for hashtags, which is extremely helpful if you know of an event that your customers are likely to attend, or if there is a particular hashtag that people in your industry use; e.g., #PRTips or
- You can use Boolean search terms such as AND and OR
- If you are looking for a set phrase, put it in quotation marks. For example, in searching for a phrase if you were a plumber, I'd probably use the phrase 'my boiler is broken'. Also, think colloquially of what is used in everyday conversation

When you do a search, it opens up to a page that gives you more options.

Once search is opened up, there are different categories:

- The default is set to top Tweets
- Live Tweets will show everybody using the particular phase or hashtag in real time, and it is in a reverse chronological order
- If you are looking for people to follow and want to find people who have your search term in their name (Twittername or Username), or in their Twitter bio, select the Accounts section
- In the 'More' section, you can look for news

- If you are a local business, you might want to choose the option of finding Tweets from people who are in a location 'Near you', which can be found in the options in the "More" tab

#2. ADVANCED SEARCH

Most people don't seem to know about Twitter's Advanced Search function. Advanced Search allows you to do more interesting and complex searches. It is not always too robust but is useful if the idea of using Boolean search seems too much for you.

You will find the language used in Advanced Search straightforward to understand. Advanced Search will allow you to search in more detail for keyword phrases, allowing you to include certain words and exclude others.

Twitter doesn't make it easy to find the Advanced Search. At the time of writing this: You get to the Advanced Search page through the search page under the 'More' tab.

> *Tip: If you think your ideal customers might ask a particular question when they are ready to buy your products or services, then tick the question box in the 'Other' section. It will select Tweets that include a question mark. This is incredibly handy.*

#3. OTHER PEOPLE

What I love about Twitter is its openness and transparency. You can learn a lot from looking at other people's profiles.

- Their followers
- Who they are following
- Lists they have created
- Lists that they are on
- Who they are talking to and their circle of friends
- Whose content they are sharing

- Which hashtags they use frequently
- The language they use in their bios may give you clues for search terms

There is a lot of information that you can get from other peoples' accounts on Twitter. A thorough investigation of a few key people can give you insights to expand your circle with the relevant people.

#4. TWITTER LISTS

Lists are probably one of the most underutilised tools that Twitter offers. Lists help you to filter your Twitter feed so that you can concentrate on people interesting to you. They also provide a great resource for finding people that other people have curated carefully into interesting categories.

When you click on a list, the default is set to seeing the filtered Twitter stream of members of the list, and you will automatically see their Tweets.

You can subscribe to lists, which is useful if someone has curated a list of people attending an event.

Click on the list members to see who is on the Twitter list. It makes it easy to follow people with a common interest. You can also add them to one of your lists.

Twitter lists are great for finding relevant people, and sometimes, companies will have lists.

For example, say you are trying to get into a big company such as Adobe. They have many lists of employees. If you start to connect with people who work for Adobe as a way of getting into a company, by forming a relationship with someone in that organisation, you can ask them for help to direct you to the right person in the company to speak to. This way, you have more chance of getting into a bigger company.

Many people have lists of local people on Twitter, which makes it easy if you're a local business to find people who are local or near to you.

> **Tip:** *It's good practice to put certain people into a List. Lists can be public or private. If you create a public list, the people within it will be notified that you have added them to a particular list. So, be mindful how you name your lists.*

#5. TWITTER ADS

This one is quite exciting, and not many talk about Twitter Ads. You don't have to pay to see the data, and you can find out:

- How many people are in your local area
- You can find out the stats on how many people are using a particular phrase or have similar interests
- You can use Twitter to target people by interests
- If someone has visited your website, you can attach a cookie to your website and target these people
- You can target people from your mailing list using Twitter Ads

I have been pleasantly surprised how much targeting you can do using Twitter Ads, and they are now more affordable to small business owners.

The main thing with Twitter Ads are the two types-of-use Twitter cards that you can create only through Twitter Ads. One of them is a Web Conversion Card, and the other a Lead Conversion Card.

> *Third Party Tools to try too:*
>
> **Followerwonk**—*This tool allows you to search by keywords and by location.*
>
> **ManageFlitter**—*The search function within this tool allows you to search bios, names, and latest Tweets.*
>
> **Twellow**—*Allows you to search for people by location and by categories.*

Case Study: Coffee Tweet leads to £14,000 Contract

EXPERT: ALAN DONEGAN

I've asked my friend, Alan Donegan, to show you how one single tweet, which was about coffee, ended up in a sizeable contract, and go through exactly what happened so that you can repeat that for your business.

One of Alan's businesses is called the Popup Business School, which helps people start small businesses quickly. He gets paid by housing associations to inspire entrepreneurship among unemployed residents through practical workshops.

From Alan:

To grow my business, I was searching for people in housing using Twitter advanced search. My major market for the Popup Business School is housing associations, and I came across an account of a director of a housing association.

Her bio said:

'Director of Housing quite enjoys a coffee.'

When I read that she quite enjoys a coffee, what do you think I said? I didn't go straight in with 'Come for coffee with me!' I tried something a bit different. I actually said:

'I love coffee too!'

And I sent her a picture of me smiling, drinking fresh Costa Rican coffee.

We chatted on Twitter about coffee, and then she sent me this Tweet:

'Just read your website, sounds really interesting. You should come in, call me tomorrow.'

I called her, and we had a brilliant chat, and she said:

'If you bring the coffee, I will get the directors of the housing association together so you can tell us about your business.'

A week and a half later, I went to visit with a bag of Costa Rican coffee. We had our chat and, by the end of the meeting, we'd done a deal for a £14,000 programme.

So, let's break this down:

Find the right person to speak to

Let's say we are looking at housing, and you find a Housing Association. Would I tweet directly to their business account?

No, because this could be a communications or marketing type person running this account for the organisation. Are these types of people going to be interested in what I'm doing? No, it's nothing to do with their day job. So I don't want to speak with the housing association; I want to speak with the people who work for it.

When you are selling your products, you don't want to sell them to the company. You want to sell them to the people who work for the company. I have found little point directly tweeting or messaging company accounts.

It is easy to find the people who work for the company using Twitter Advanced Search. Just start searching for the company name, job titles, positions, interests related to your product, or anything you think will identify the customer you want.

You can also go to LinkedIn and search for a decision maker by job title and then find them on Twitter; that's a fantastic route.

Find something that you have in common to talk about

Twitter is powerful. The reason it's so powerful is that it is still free to contact anyone. If you want to contact the director of a business, someone specific in the company, or if you want to contact the person in charge of the health and wellbeing programme for a particular housing association, you can find those people. We can reach out and talk to them and say the equivalent of, 'I like coffee too' based on whatever is in their bio.

Get their attention

If you get a random message from someone, saying, 'I like coffee too,' what is the first thing you are going to think?

Weirdo, who on earth is Alan Donegan?

While there is a chance that people might ignore the Tweet, I tend to find that people will click on your profile, wondering who the hell you are.

This is what happened with the Housing Association Director. She thought, 'Who the hell is this guy?' Then she clicked on my profile, which at the time, said we worked with housing associations. She thought that sounded interesting and so she clicked on the link below the bio, which went to my website. She had a look at my website and decided to tweet me back and talk to me.

Notice that I didn't go straight in with, 'Let's have a coffee' or 'buy my service'.

Be interested in them first

You have got to join the conversation about whatever the person is talking about, and then they will go 'who is this person?' and probably check you out. Then, if they are interested in what you are doing, they will find out more. If they are not, they won't. But it is the quickest way to get in touch with people who might be interested in your business.

I send lots of messages to other people saying, what do you think about this, or what is going on. Sometimes, they ignore me or, sometimes, they show interest back.

I see Twitter as a giant online networking space, and I would never do anything on Twitter that I wouldn't do in real life. Once you have gotten them started in conversation, they will check out your profile and bio. The bio is the bit where they will decide whether it is interesting enough to click on your website or not. It has to be interesting. If it is all business, there is little for me to connect to. If there is a bit of personality or other stuff, then that is what you can connect with.

Twitter is the most incredibly quick tool to find customers who might be interested in your product that you can talk to.

You can chat without following, but just following is sometimes enough for people to wonder who is following them. I prefer to follow them and send them a message if I want to talk to them because they get a notification, and you can create a conversation.

It depends on the value of your contract as well. So, if you are going for contracts and you only need, for example, ten contracts to keep you going for the entire year, then you want to contact people individually and create individual relationships.

If you need 50,000 clients to keep you going for the year, then it's nearly impossible to create 50,000 individual connections. You will need other customers to spread the word on Twitter for you.

Individuals buy your product, the individuals make the decision, and the individuals will support you in what you are doing. Twitter allows you to directly contact and talk to individuals you would have never met any other way.

Make sure your bio is relevant and interesting

Although my bio now says something different, at the time I approached the director, my bio said:

'We work with housing associations to help their residents start small businesses and make money doing what they love.'

The bio was relevant to her and, because of this, she clicked through to my website.

It's useful to freshen up your bio. I sometimes change my website link too, so for example, if I am promoting an event, my link will be changed to the event's page on my website. Keep it current depending on the type of people you are focused on contacting.

ALAN'S TIPS FOR FINDING THE RIGHT PEOPLE:

- Find people with certain keywords in their bio with Advanced Search on Twitter
- Find local people—look for local accounts, newspapers, weather accounts (only local people are interested in local weather), village accounts, and relevant hashtags
- Find people who follow products related to yours. So, for example, let's say you were selling cookies; what goes with cookies? Coffee! So, where do you find a list of geographically-based people who drink coffee? Why not look for local coffee shops and see who is following them
- Find people talking about a related experience or product by listening on Social Media and searching for keywords
- Conference crashing; there is bound to be a conference in your industry for what you do. Find out the hashtag. You can see everyone who tweets with that hashtag and join the conversation without even leaving your house. Just searching the hashtag for the Annual Housing Association Conference has generated all sorts of contacts for me

---

Alan's Top Tip: Save time on Twitter by finding the right people quickly and talking directly to the people who might actually buy your services, and stop all the other stuff that takes up so much time.

Thank you, Alan.

Good Practices to Get into a New Corporate

Set up Google Alerts for mentions of the company, and alerts on Mentions or Talkwalker, too.

Be on the lookout for news that suggests changes are taking place with the organisation, such as:

- New funding
- Recruiting, which could indicate growth, or could indicate a high turnover of staff
- Job changes
- Relocation news
- New launches of products and services

Look out for events where you could meet some of the employees in real life.

Go through their website thoroughly:

- Read their blog content
- Do they have a page that mentions people working there?
- Subscribe to their newsletter
- Do they have links to Social Media on their website?

Google the Company Name:

- See what other people are saying about the company
- On review sites
- In comments

Go to their LinkedIn Company Page:

- Follow their page
- Read the content they're posting

- Look at all the employees linked to the Company Page—how are you connected? Which people look interesting?

Look at Employees' LinkedIn Profiles:

- Do they have a Twitter account?—Follow them
- Which groups do they belong to?—Could you join any of these groups?
- Who has given them recommendations? (Look for suppliers and customers)
- What reason could you have to connect with them?
- When you connect with them, make sure you tag them (they won't see how you've tagged them) and add notes and set a reminder to contact them

Do an Advanced Search on LinkedIn:

- For people currently working for the company—not everyone will link to the Company Page
- For people who have worked for the company in the past—are you connected with any of them? Is it worth ringing any of them to find out more about the company

Go to the Company's Twitter Account:

- Are there related Twitter accounts?
- Have a look at the type of content they are tweeting
- Are there any hashtags they use frequently?
- Are they retweeting other people's content?
- Is their content only about them?
- Look for interactions with others
- Look at who they follow and who follows them
- Look at whether they have any Lists—sometimes companies may have a list of employees or news sources that they follow

Find Employees on Twitter:

- Follow the people that you have seen from LinkedIn that have a Twitter account
- Do a Twitter search on the company name and look at the accounts that come up
- Follow them
- See if they have any useful lists—they may have lists of people who work for their company
- What are they talking about and with whom do they interact? Is their Twitter business related?
- Add employees to a private Twitter List (they won't know that you have added them to the list)

Do a search on Twitter for the company name, both by the name of the company in inverted commas and by their Twitter name:

- Look at who is talking about the company and what they are saying
- Is it positive or negative? Do they have a customer issue? Or are they great at customer service?
- Which other companies are talking about them?

Find their Facebook Page:

- What are they posting?
- How do they respond to comments?

Go to YouTube and do a search on the Company Name:

- Do they have a YouTube Channel?
- What type of videos do they post?
- Is anyone non-company related talking about them?

Go to Instagram and search for their Company Name:

- Follow it

- Look for events and announcements
- Look for pictures of employees at events

Set up a tab on Hootsuite for the company with different streams so that you can monitor conversations and look for opportunities to engage.

Take Action with the information that you have gathered.

Start talking to people who work for the company without selling anything or pitching your business.

Gather information to find the right group of people to speak to. Most businesses have 3 – 6 people involved in the buying process.

Create content that would be useful and helpful.

> *Tip: Offer Value when you approach the right person. If you have researched properly, you should have a way to offer value to them.*

Practical: How to Create a

Twitter List Automatically

Twitter chats are great fun, and it is a brilliant way to network and meet new people. But what happens after the hour is over? Have you ever tried to find all the people taking part in a particular Twitter chat and add them to a list? It can take a lot of time if the chat has been busy. Perhaps, you would like to follow people attending an event which has a particular hashtag. You can create these lists manually, but there is a simpler way.

Here's a step-by-step guide to using an app called IFTTT to set up a rule so that each time someone Tweets using a hashtag or your keyword search, they will automatically be put into a Twitter list that you have created. Like magic! IFTTT stands for If This Then That. It is a great way to automate some of your workflow. It took me a while to warm to IFTTT, as a non-techy person, but it is incredibly useful, and I will show you how to create a recipe easily.

1. Sign up if you haven't already to IFTTT and make sure you connect your Twitter account. Ideally, you want to connect all your platforms, but for this exercise, we just need your Twitter account

2. Go to My Recipes, under the IF tab, and you will find a 'Create a Recipe' button. Click on it

3. Click on the blue word 'this'. This creates the first part of the recipe. What we want to happen is that every time the Twitter chat hashtag is used, it creates a trigger for the recipe to be used

4. Choose Twitter as the 'Trigger Channel'. You can do this either by scrolling through all the icons and finding the Twitter one or by simply typing Twitter in the search bar

5. Choose 'New Tweet from Search' as the Trigger

6. Add your Twitter hashtag or search terms. Put phrases in quote marks. If you use multiple keywords, separate them with 'OR'
7. You are now going to create a rule for what happens when someone uses that hashtag or search term. Click on the blue word 'that'
8. Choose Twitter as your 'Action Channel'
9. Choose 'Add User to a list' as the Action
10. Don't touch the Username. It is automatically correct for the list to be created in your Twitter account
11. Create a list name. Click on the 'Create Action' button
12. Check that you are happy with the recipe and click 'Create Recipe'

And that's it: you're done. From now on, whenever someone uses the hashtag that you have set up, they will automatically be added to the list that you have just created.

Note:

You can create this recipe to create a Twitter List for any hashtag or search term that is useful to you

People notice when you add them to a list

The recipe can be switched off at any time too

If you automate adding people to a list, make sure you declutter your list. Because some spammers will use popular hashtags

If you are using this for a chat, set it up beforehand so that all the people in the chat are automatically added to the list

Part 3 - Nurture

It would be lovely if all you had to do was send out a single Tweet or LinkedIn post to get a new customer. The reality is that it takes time and several points of contact. In this section we will focus on building longer-term relationships online.

Fairy Tales

We're brought up on fairy tales of boy meets girl (sometimes they're princes and princesses), they have a bit of an adventure, and then get married and live happily ever after.

However, we all know that relationships in the real world are vastly different. The marriage is just the start of the relationship. While not all marriages last happily ever after, most last longer than the courtship period. And some would last longer if the partners spent the same amount of care and attention as during courtship.

Looking back at the start of the relationship: You don't ask for marriage on the first date. The courtship period helps you to get to know each other better. Often, it is the small gestures that make the big difference to building that relationship.

If the courtship is successful, at some point there will be a proposal to take the relationship to the next level.

CHAPTER 6

Nurture Your Existing Customers

Social Media is incredibly useful to help you find new customers, and we go into more detail later about how to do that on LinkedIn and Twitter, but don't forget your existing customers.

It is five times more profitable to spend money on retaining existing customers than it is to acquire new ones. Usually, customers leave you because they don't feel that you care about them. Research has shown that 66% of customers will leave because of an attitude of indifference toward them from the owner, manager, or an employee.

How well do you know your existing customers?

In the Personal Branding chapter, I created a worksheet for you to complete that will help you to understand your customers better. If you skipped over filling it in, now would be a good time to go back and complete it. Some of the questions help you think about what you are doing with your existing customers and what you're doing to retain them. How often do you interact with them? Social Media allows you to engage with existing customers as well as find new ones.

Another reason to focus in on your customers is that they give you a great insight into the type of business you're attracting at the moment. I am always surprised how many business owners tell me that their customers aren't their ideal customers. Or how many people tell me that they market to everyone.

If you try to market to everyone, you end up reaching no one.

Too often, business owners are not clear enough about who their customers are. When I have worked with clients, too frequently, they've given me vague answers like anyone or everyone buying a house or anyone from a six-month-old to a ninety-five-year-old. This type of marketing is called 'spray and pray', where you hope that if you offer your services to as big a group as possible that some of it will stick.

Your customers are not everyone who could use your product; they are the people who are most likely to buy your product or service.

For example, if you are selling a sealant product for a car, not everyone who drives a car will buy your product. If you have a new car, you are unlikely to need a sealant product. If you prefer a mechanic to fix your car, you are unlikely to use a sealant product. People with older cars, who like looking under the bonnet and enjoy fixing their cars, are the most obvious group to target, or the mechanics themselves.

Being niche makes it easier for you to establish yourself as the go-to person in your area of expertise. The clearer you are about what you do or sell, the easier it will be for your customers to know that you are the right person for them. The easier it is for other people to recommend you to the right person who needs your product or service.

I used to market pet food for Spillers Pet Foods, which is now part of Nestle. We had two customers that we needed to consider for marketing, the pet, and their owner. Ultimately, the product had to satisfy the pet. No owner would continue to buy a product that their cat or dog wouldn't eat, or if it caused problems with their digestive system, let's say. The product had to be both nutritious and tasty. And, no dog or cat could try our products without their owners buying the products for them. So we had to focus on marketing to pet owners and making it appealing to them. That also depended on how they saw their pet. To some people, it was an animal, and to others, a member of the family, and to some, a child substitute. However, the pet owners (and animals) were not our only customers. They needed to be able to find our products with ease. The retailers that stocked our product in their stores were also our customers and our sales department, focused on building relationships with retailers and wholesalers.

You may have two or more customers: your end user and the person who will buy from you. The buyer may not even use your product/ software/ services. The purchaser will ask quite different questions than your end-users would.

You can't appeal to everyone, and that's okay. Very few big brands have universal appeal. You want the people that you appeal to, to love your product or service so that they can recommend it to the relevant people. If you adapt your service to every new customer, you are likely to over-promise and under-deliver. You will send out mixed messages.

Defining an ideal customer doesn't mean that all your customers have to be your ideal customer, but it will help you to focus on where to spend your time and energy.

Know your buyers' need

Is there a problem you can solve? What does your customer need or want that you can help them to achieve? Selling products or services is not about you and your business or products you offer, but ultimately, about your customer. If they don't see the need for your product or service, they won't buy from you. Remember, you are not a mind reader, and asking great questions will help you get to know your potential customer better.

You need to have some way of qualifying people to find out if they are likely to be your customers now or in the future.

Many sales professionals use a system called BANT to qualify potential customers:

- Do they have the **B**udget to buy?

- Do they have the **A**uthority to buy?

- Do they have the **N**eed to buy?

- Where are they on the buying **T**imeline?

I am not suggesting that you only talk to people who will buy from you. Rather, that by assessing potential customers, you can make the decision about how to invest your time best for your business. It is nice to spend time with your peers and, yes, you will learn from them and, yes, some of them will recommend you, but if you feel that you don't have enough time, and you need more hours in a day, then spending that time with potential and existing customers will pay higher dividends for your business.

What is your customer experience like at the moment?

If your products or services are rubbish right now, then Social Media won't solve things. You need to get your house in order first. What is your customer experience like at every point of contact? What do you do pre-sales? What do they think when they visit your website? How easy is it to buy from you? Do you follow up consistently? Do you get feedback from your customers after the sale? Do you keep in touch with your customers regularly?

Social Media gives you an ideal opportunity to speak directly to potential customers, to research new ideas and to keep top-of-mind for your customers. It is worth thinking about what systems you are going to have in place to keep in contact with your customers and how you are going to keep in touch. Do you have a mailing list that potential customers can subscribe to if they find you via Social Media so that you can nurture a relationship with them until they feel ready to buy?

It's worth doing a quick audit if you can be completely neutral, or ask someone outside the business to give you a review as a potential client. And, it's always worth asking customers what they think you should:

STOP doing,

START doing,

CONTINUE to do.

The Classic Buying Journey

To understand your customers' buying journey, it is useful to start thinking about how you go about buying new things first. As a business owner, you need to think like a consumer. It will help you to stop selling and start helping your customers to buy from you. Marketing and advertising people use an acronym (AIDA) to describe a common list of events that may occur when a consumer makes a decision to purchase:

Attention—Interest—Desire—Action

Here's a slightly different version often used in marketing:

Awareness—Interest—Evaluation—Decision—Action—

Referral—Loyalty

It's a simplified system to give you a general understanding of how to target a market effectively. Obviously, as you move from step to step, you lose some people.

- **Awareness**: Your customer first needs to be aware of your product. Attract the attention of the customer. If your customer doesn't know that you exist, you will never sell a product or service to them, no matter how fabulous your product or services are

- **Interest**: Your customer needs to be interested in your product or service. They know they have a problem that they want to solve, but they may not know how to solve it. Think about it. If you think of yourself as a travel adventurer, who likes to go off the beaten track, you may be aware of cruise liner companies, but would you be interested in a cruise line holiday advertisement?

- **Evaluation**: They will go through a period of evaluation. Your customer is aware of their problem and is committed to spending time and effort to come up with a potential solution. This may be a few seconds for low-price items like choosing a brand of chocolate, or could last weeks; e.g., for which car to buy, or even years for software systems

- **Decision**: At some point, they will make a decision to buy. By this stage, they will have thoroughly researched their problems and potential decisions, but they may not have decided which company they will use yet. Your customers need to be convinced that they want and desire your product or service and that it will satisfy their needs

- **Action**: Create an action, such as make a phone call or subscribe to your mailing list or make a purchase. Never underestimate the customer experience at this point. Most buyers will experience some feeling of remorse and doubts that they have made the right decision straight after purchase

- **Referral**: After the Purchase, if they are happy, they may make a referral by filling in a review or recommending you to someone. Customer reviews are important for new customers

- **Loyalty**: If you offer them a great customer experience, you have the opportunity to build loyalty so that they are more likely to buy from you again. Move them from being one-off customers to regular customers or clients

Make Your Existing Customers Your First Priority

Your existing customers are of vital importance. Frequently, businesses focus most of their marketing budget on acquiring new customers and too little on marketing to their existing customers. Customer loyalty and retention drive revenue and referral. When you satisfy a customer, you reduce your churn rate. Nurturing your relationship with existing customers is important and shouldn't be forgotten in the quest for new customers.

Some figures:

- It costs five times more to acquire a new customer than satisfying and retaining existing customers   (Alan E Webber, 'B2B Customer Experience Priorities In an Economic Downturn: Key Customer Usability Initiatives In A Soft Economy,' Forrester Research, February 19, 2008)
- Reducing churn rate on your customers by 5% can increase your profits by between 25 to 125%
- The probability of selling to an existing customer is 60 – 70%. The probability of selling to a new customer is 5 – 20% (Market Metrics Study)
- Customers are more likely to switch companies because they feel unsatisfied with the service than because they have a problem with the product
- According to Accenture Strategy 2015 Global Consumer Pulse Research:

> *52% of consumers have switched providers in the past year due to poor customer service. 81% of consumers admit that it is frustrating dealing with a company that does not make it easy to do business with them. Once a provider loses a customer, 68% of consumers will not go back. 80% of 'switchers' felt that the company could have done something to retain them.*

Why You Need Social Media for Customer Care

One of the big fears that stops many people from going on Twitter is that someone will say bad things about them. The problem with avoiding Twitter is that people will be talking about you whether you are there or not. And, you will never know.

- You may even be pleasantly surprised and hear lovely things about you
- People will be more likely to share their positive experiences about you if they can see that you have a Twitter account
- People also make pre-sale enquiries through Twitter, which you will miss out on if you don't have a Twitter account
- Negative Feedback is good too
- 95% of unhappy customers will never complain, and so, the 5% of dissatisfied customers that do complain, are like gold dust

They help you understand where problems are. You may be blissfully unaware that your customers are having problems with one of the following: your website, products, services, or other parts of the customer experience. Most customers will just leave if they feel unhappy with your service and neglected.

Negative feedback allows you an opportunity to put things right.

95% of customers whose problems were resolved quickly stated that they would buy from the supplier again. Customers who complain and are satisfied are up to 8% more loyal than if they had no problem at all (1988, John Goodman TARP).

USING SOCIAL MEDIA FOR CUSTOMER CARE

The majority of customers prefer human interaction over digital. According to Accenture Strategy 2015 Global Consumer Pulse Research, 73% of UK consumers will choose a human over digital capability when seeking advice or looking to resolve a service issue or complaint. (I wonder if 'digital capability' included automated-telephone-options?) This suggests that most of your customers will speak to or email you directly, but you can't ignore Social Media.

A third of Social Media users prefer Social Care to the telephone. According to research by the Institute of Customer Service, complaints on Social Media increased eight-fold during 2015.

Most people will ask questions, comment, and complain via Facebook. This is not surprising considering that the bulk of people use Facebook. If you have a Facebook Page, you need to respond to people there. The problem with Facebook is that if people complain on their Facebook personal profile, it is almost impossible to find. The perk of people using Twitter is that tweets are public, and you can search and find all mentions of your business whether or not they use your Twitter username.

The advantage of Twitter is that:

- Tweets are public and visible, which means you can find complaints, praise, and feedback. Anyone can watch how you respond to your customers
- Tweets are conversational and concise
- Testimonials or 'Twestimonials' can be amplified on Twitter and can be embedded into your website as social proof
- You can have real-time conversations with customers
- You can improve customer experience and satisfaction. A bit of humour can take customer service to a completely different level. In June 2014, a customer complained with a fish pun, which led to two fish-pun-filled hours between him and the Sainsbury's Twitter account. The interaction was reported on news channels and in the major newspapers, resulting in a lot of positive Public Relations for Sainsbury's. If you want to see the interaction on Twitter, here it is:
  https://twitter.com/teaandcopy/timelines/421628995365388288

- You have an opportunity to get real insights into what your customers want by getting involved in discussions
- Costs of dealing with customers can be 80% less per interaction than by phone
- Being seen to be available for customer care means that you are also available for new enquiries and opportunities

---

Best Practices for Customer Care Using Twitter

Unless you have a high volume of customer enquiries via Twitter, I would recommend that you deal with customer care on your main Twitter account. Most small businesses that I've worked with find managing a single Twitter account enough of a challenge. There is a chance that if you set up a separate account, and it doesn't have much activity, that you won't check it on a daily basis.

Respond.—Believe it or not, 40% of Tweets to customer service accounts don't get a response. 81% of consumers do not recommend a brand to their friends if the brand did not respond to their enquiries. Enough said.

Respond quickly.—People expect a response quickly from Social Media. They may be more forgiving if they know you are a small local business, but only responding during business hours may lead to lost opportunities and frustrated customers. If someone asks you a question, and you take 24hrs to respond, there is a good chance that they will already have a response. *From a competitor!*

Be human.—If you are using your company account with a business logo, sign each of the Tweets with your name so that the person knows that you are a human being, and use informal language. According to Twitter's research: 83% of customers with personalised interaction felt satisfied with their customer service experience on Twitter, and 77% were likely to recommend the brand to others.

Empathise.—with your customer. Match the language and tone of the Tweet. Although, if they are shouting (all capitals), I don't suggest you shout back, but you can add an exclamation mark.

Solve their problem or move them offline.—So that you can have a proper conversation. I'm lucky that I've been blogging for a long time, so a lot of the questions that I'm asked, I've already written a blog about. It is easy for me to share a link to answer the question. If people ask you the same question a few times, it is useful to create content to help answer the query. It is important that you are seen to respond, so make sure that even if you have their contact details and give them a call, you also respond on Twitter. A simple Tweet, saying something like, I'm giving you a call, or, I'm sending you a DM, will reassure observers that you are dealing with their problem.

Make it easy for people to send you a private message.—Consider making your Direct Messages available to anyone if you get many customer service tweets, or you need confidential information from your customers. This allows people to send you private messages without having to wait for you to follow them.

Make it Easy for Customers to Send You a Private Message

Twitter has only introduced this recently, and it isn't that obvious but is easy when you know how. Do this from Twitter.com because the Twitter app doesn't have all the options.

- Enable anyone to send you a message: Go into your Settings, click on Privacy, and then tick the box to allow anyone to send you a Direct Message
- While you are in Settings, find out what your Twitter ID number is. In your Settings, look for 'Your Twitter Data', click on that, and you will find your number
- Copy the number and insert it after the '=' sign (see below) https://twitter.com/messages/compose?recipient_id={your account's numeric user ID}
- This is the link you can use within a Tweet, which will create a call to action button, which says, '*Send me a Private Message*. You are welcome to send me a Tweet @NickyKriel if you want to test it out so that you can see what the Tweet looks like. I don't mind being experimented on

> *Tip: Keep this link in a handy place so that you can use it when you need it. I find that sending myself a DM is a useful place to store links on Twitter.*

Connect with People You Already Know

If you have enough business, and have business enquiries coming in each day, you probably don't need to expand the group of people that you know. If you need more customers, you will need to either increase the number of people in your network or spend more time interacting with the people you know already. Or both. Most business will come from connections just outside your immediate network. Ideally, people you know well, and who have worked with you, will recommend you to people looking for your product, skills, or service. However, in reality, you will need to work on relationships to keep yourself top-of-mind within your network. You will also have to make contact with people that you haven't yet met. Having ten or twenty connections on LinkedIn or Twitter won't help you that much. It is not so much the people you know, as the people they might know. The bigger your network, the more opportunities you have. But, remember, there is no point in just collecting people for the sake of numbers. You want to build a quality network of people that know, like, and trust you.

LinkedIn makes it easy for you to reconnect with people you know already. Each year of your life, you meet new people.

So whom do you already know that you haven't connected with yet?

- Past colleagues
- People who were at school or university with you
- People you have met networking (do you have a pile of business cards somewhere?)
- People on your mailing list or contact list
- People you meet through social events or shared interests

When was the last time you contacted some of your connections? I know someone who met up with an old colleague for a quick cup of coffee to stay in touch and walked away with eighteen days of training.

So often, we forget about the people we know already. The people you have been with at university, college, or even from your first job. Often, we lose touch with people we like because life gets in the way. They might be in exactly the right position to do business with you. How often do you reconnect with people that you knew in the past? You can wait for a chance encounter to bump into them, or you can reach out to them via LinkedIn.

Quite frequently, you will know people and socialise. You will know their children, and what their habits are, but you won't know what they do or what business they are in—because we don't ask those questions. So, LinkedIn is usually quite useful for finding out about people you know through social events and shared interest, and they are likely to accept your invitation to connect because they know you already.

One of the companies that I have worked for was Spillers Pet Food, which has been bought out by Nestlé. LinkedIn matched me with somebody that I used to work with at Spillers. He had been in a more senior position than me, but we got on well. He had gone onto doing training for Nestle Europe and was based in Godalming, which is close to where I live in Guildford. We hadn't seen each other for 15 years, if not longer, and we didn't have to sell to each other because we knew and liked one another. I wouldn't have thought to contact him, but felt delighted when his invitation to connect came through. We have met up and now keep in touch.

There are always people that you know who are better at connecting people than others. Even in a friendship group, there are certain people who introduce more people into the group. It is always worth thinking about who your connectors are, and make sure that you nurture the relationship.

When was the last time you thanked them?

Chapter 7

Nurture New Connections— Start with 'Hello'

There is no point in just finding interesting people. The first step in any relationship is saying hello. This chapter will cover the connecting etiquette for both LinkedIn and Twitter.

Connecting Etiquette on LinkedIn

If you have a LinkedIn account, I am sure that you will be familiar with getting a standard invitation from a person you don't know. Do you connect or not connect?

On the other hand, I am sure that you have looked at someone interesting that you potentially would like to do business with or someone you respect in your industry, yet you don't know them personally. Do you send them an invite to connect, or do you leave it?

I thought it would be useful to go through some LinkedIn connecting etiquette.

Remember, there is no absolutely fixed and hard rule, and it is up to you to decide personally which approach you will take.

Completely closed to completely open networking

You can choose only to connect with people that you have actually met.

- May seem sensible because, if someone asks you about one of your connections, you can give an informed answer
- If someone looks at your connections, they will show a fair reflection on you
- LinkedIn suggests that you only ask people that you know to connect with them
- However, there are serious limitations taking this approach
- Think about it, if you went to a networking meeting, would you only talk to people you had already met?
- Your search on LinkedIn is limited if you only have a few connections—you will only be shown your 1st, 2nd, and 3rd connections and people in your Groups when you search on LinkedIn
- You are less likely to be found in LinkedIn Search if you have only a few connections

On the other extreme, there is a group of people called LIONs (which stands for LinkedIn Open Networkers).

- Their mission is to be connected with the largest number of people possible
- They seek quantity rather than quality of connections
- You will just be a number to them
- They are unlikely to know anything about their connections

I don't believe that you should take this approach either. I believe that if you think of LinkedIn as a form of networking, you will have the right approach to it. Connect with people you know and would like to know better.

Tips for Connecting on LinkedIn

#1 TO CONNECT OR NOT TO CONNECT

Accepting connections

This is my approach to accepting connections, which you may find useful:

- Connect with everyone I know in real life unless I don't like them (Okay, I'm human!)
- Connect with everyone who has given me a personalised invitation to connect
- All local business people, whether or not they send me a personalised invitation—there is a good chance that we will have a mutual acquaintance, and it is easy to meet for a coffee
- Connect with most people in the same industry, whether or not they send me a personalised invitation
- Extremely cautious about invitations that come from other countries in unrelated industries
- Don't accept invitations from profiles that lack photos and that are barely filled in, or filled in badly, unless I know the person
- Don't accept invitations from people that show an inability to communicate in English. I don't expect perfect grammar when it's obvious that English is not a person's first language, but I want reassurances that we will be able to have a conversation
- Don't accept invitations when there are strong indicators that the person may send me an inappropriate advance. Yes, some people seem to think that LinkedIn is a dating site (and the same with Facebook, too)
- I prefer to give most people the benefit of the doubt because I can always disconnect them if they send me spam or a marriage proposal

It is up to you what criteria you use.

Sending connections

Always, always give someone a reason to connect with you (unless you press a button which sends the invitation too quickly, of course). However, it is better to send an invitation to connect with someone that you would like to speak to than spending hours thinking about how to personalise the invite and not doing it.

#2 HOW TO CONNECT—PERSONALISED INVITE

LinkedIn allows you the following options when you connect:

- Colleague
- Classmate
- We've done business together
- Friend
- Other
- I don't know X

Obviously, if you are colleagues or alumni, or have worked together in the past, then choose those options. If you have their email address because you have their business card, you can choose 'Other'. I tend to choose 'Friend', which allows me to connect without their email address, but then I explain why I want to meet them.

Ideally, your invitation should:

- Remind them how you know each other (if you have met them networking, remind them of the event)
- If you have never met in real life, let them know how you know about them
- Give them a reason to connect with you
- Try to find at least one positive thing to say about them. We all like compliments
- Do not try to sell anything at all in the invitation

- You have only a limited number of characters, so make sure you use them well

---

Note:

If you connect via the mobile app, your connection request will be sent immediately, and you don't have to say how you know each other and won't have a chance to personalise the message.

LinkedIn also suggests people that you might know; if you connect this way, the invitation to connect gets sent automatically and, again, you won't be able to personalise the message.

#3 WHEN TO CONNECT

In most cases, if you give the person a good reason to connect, they will.

- Good to connect with someone as soon you find him or her on LinkedIn. It is so easy to find an excuse to delay connecting, which ends up meaning that you don't end up connecting. The best time is the present
- Sometimes, you might want to see if you can get a conversation going with the person first by connecting with them on Twitter
- Find a group they belong to and interact with them there
- If someone has produced a blog or published an article on LinkedIn, leave a well thought through comment and then, shortly afterward, send an invitation mentioning that you enjoyed the article

#4 HOW TO MAKE SURE YOU SEND A PERSONALISED MESSAGE

It is so easy to send a standard invitation by accident. LinkedIn makes it too easy to press a connect button. If you use the mobile app, it is almost impossible to send a personal invitation unless you are highly observant. On LinkedIn.com, the best way to make sure that you send a personal invitation is from the person's profile.

Don't judge anyone too harshly for sending a standard invite.

- They may have pushed a button to connect and not been given the option to personalise it
- LinkedIn makes it far too easy to send an impersonal invitation, especially if you're using the app
- I have sent standard invitations by mistake
- Some of my best business opportunities started with receiving an impersonal invitation to connect
- It is better to send a standard invitation than to dither and not send the invitation at all

#5 WHEN TO CONTACT A PERSON

It is useful to get in touch quickly, especially if you had a strong reason for connecting. I've seen recommendations that you should reply immediately with an introduction of your business, but I don't agree. Be wary of pitching your business too soon. When new connections try to sell to me as soon as I connect, it puts me off. Think of it as starting a conversation.

Do not sell to new connections as soon as you have said hello.

- Thank them for connecting
- Ask them questions about their business first
- Send them information that will be useful to them
- If the connection is your ideal customer, the intention of messaging is to get the connection to agree to a phone call or meeting, and not to sell to them via InMail

In many cases, the connection will be to start a relationship that can, potentially, be beneficial to both of you in the future.

How to Use Referrals to Connect with People

Inbuilt referrals

There is a function on LinkedIn, which is called 'referrals'.

If you don't know someone and are not connected with them, you can ask somebody who is connected with them to refer you or recommend you.

Some LinkedIn trainers recommend that you use referrals as a way of getting visibility and building relationships.

Personally, I recommend that you ask the person directly by sending them a personalised invitation and give them a reason you want to connect. It has worked for me. It also eliminates the chance of annoying your contacts if they get many referral requests.

Old school

You can also do something that most people forget about:

If you see that one of your friends is connected to somebody that you want to be connected with, pick up the phone or send an email. Just because it's online, it doesn't mean you have to keep things on LinkedIn.

Don't forget, you know that person, and it is a good excuse to have a telephone conversation. You never know what might happen in that 'hello-nice-to-catch-up-and-can-you-connect-me-to-this-person?' conversation.

- It will give you more information about that person (good and bad)
- They may give you the person's number and tell you the best way to contact them
- They may help you connect to them

- The conversation might remind them to put you in touch with someone else
- It might remind them of an upcoming opportunity

The choice is yours.

Using Groups

Find mutual connections and send them a quick email to ask if they mind you using their name to connect.

Benefits of doing this:

- Reminds your acquaintance that you are around
- Great opportunity to find out more about the connection
- It shows respect that you are not abusing your connection
- You are not asking for anything from your acquaintance but a simple 'yes'
- If the person you're trying to connect with speaks to your acquaintance, they will have had recent contact with you
- Even though all you are asking is whether they mind you using their name, they may offer to introduce you or suggest other people too

Find a shared group that both you and your potential group belong to already or join a group.

- Reach out to the person via the shared group with a message

WHAT TO WRITE IN YOUR INTRODUCTORY MESSAGE:

- That both of you are connected to your mutual acquaintance
- How you know your acquaintance

- That you have asked your acquaintance whether to connect with them and that they thought it would be a good connection. (Your acquaintance would have objected if they didn't think it was)
- It would be nice to chat and find out about their business or what they are working on at the moment
- Suggest a time for a talk

Benefits of doing this:

- Highly likely to agree to connect
- You are offering social proof that you are worth connecting to
- You are showing that you're interested in them
- More open to having a conversation with you
- Do Not Sell when you approach someone to connect
- Your call to action is having a conversation
- By suggesting a time, you are adding urgency to your message

Connecting Etiquette for Twitter

Follow them.

Send them a Tweet.

It is that simple!

(In the 'Inspiration for Twitter' in the Attract section, I suggested a few ways to introduce yourself on Twitter.)

CHAPTER 8

Nurture Relationships Until They are Ready

I t's all very well finding and connecting with people, but there is no point collecting contacts if you have no intention of taking that relationship further. Nurturing relationships is important for business. You cannot just put a Tweet out there and expect to get business because people need to get to know you in some way. Some people will do business on their first contact, but most need reassurance that they can trust you.

It's crucial to put in the soft touches first on Social Media. Get to know and be nice to people, give them useful information, and be helpful and part of the community. Of course, as a business, you need to get the sale, but you will get better results if you give freely first. I suggest that you use a one-in-five ratio of talking about your business versus giving helpful information, having conversations, and sharing other people's content. There is no point in being nice and chatty all the time you are on Social Media; you do need to do business, and generally, people will accept this if you have already built up a long and strong relationship.

Nurturing relationships are important, and you do that by:

- Engaging people through conversations
- Sharing other people's content
- Helping. People remember how you make them feel

178

- Introducing people. Connect people with each other
- Staying top-of-mind. So, it's not just putting a Tweet out there, and then, five months later, coming back to it wondering if any conversation has happened. You need always to be seen to be on Social Media, and it doesn't have to take up too much time if you are organised

---

30 Social Selling Triggers on LinkedIn

Gerry Moran kindly gave me permission to reproduce his list of 30 Social Selling Triggers. Originally, this list was published on Marketing Think.com:

https://marketingthink.com/30-linkedin-social-selling-sales-triggers/

Gerry Moran is a Global Social Media & Content Marketer, and was listed in Forbes Top 40 Social Marketing Talent.

The Social Selling Triggers give you permission to reach out to current or future members of your network:

1. Your LinkedIn profile is viewed
2. You receive an invitation to LinkedIn
3. Contact accepts your invitation to LinkedIn
4. Contact changes a job
5. Contact gets a promotion
6. Contact has a birthday
7. Contact has a work anniversary
8. Contact is mentioned in the news
9. Contact updates something in their profile—photo, summary, etc.
10. Your LinkedIn blog post is liked

11. Your LinkedIn blog post is shared
12. LinkedIn blog post is commented on
13. Daily update is liked
14. Daily update is shared
15. Daily update is commented on
16. Group post is liked
17. Group post is shared
18. Group post is commented on
19. Group member makes a comment in a group
20. You are endorsed for a skill
21. You are recommended by a contact
22. You have an opportunity to ask for a recommendation from a contact
23. You are invited to join a LinkedIn group
24. A shared group member reaches out to you
25. You receive an InMail
26. A contact's contact likes a LinkedIn update post
27. A contact's contact comments on a LinkedIn update post
28. A contact's contact shares a LinkedIn update post
29. Your contact writes a LinkedIn blog post
30. LinkedIn's 'People You May Know' feature presents a contact that is connected to someone in your network

Thank you, Gerry Moran.

25 Ways to Stay Top-of-Mind on Twitter

Assuming that you have added key people to Twitter Lists so that you can pay attention to them, there is no point in just watching their stream and never interacting. Below, are ways that you can remind potential and existing customers that you are around. These are small touches that will help build relationships on Twitter:

1. Tweet at least one good piece of relevant content every day
2. If they have just followed you, thank them with more than a 'Thank you for following me'. There are so many automated bots that they might think you've automated the thank you
3. Retweet them. This pushes their content to your audience
4. Quote Retweet them, adding a comment
5. Retweet them by replying, adding 'RT' in front of their name and copying their Tweet. This makes it more obvious that you have shared their content
6. Add them to a Public list with a flattering name. You can add the same person to numerous lists
7. Reply to one of their Tweets
8. Tweet them—anything
9. Tag them to a link—make sure the post is relevant
10. Tag them to an image with words. Again, make sure the image is relevant
11. Tag them to a photo
12. Mention them in a tweet
13. #FF them on Friday. #FF is a hashtag used on a Friday to suggest people to follow. Make sure you give a reason people should follow them. Plenty of different hashtags exist that you can use on different days; keep your eyes open
14. Give them a shout out
15. Like their Tweet
16. Send them a personalised video
17. Send them a DM

18. Create a group DM for a discussion (No sales pitches!)
19. Thank them for retweeting
20. Introduce them to someone on Twitter
21. Share their LinkedIn Published post on Twitter. Make sure that you include their Twitter name
22. Share a blog post from their website
23. Ask them a question—anything
24. Join a Twitter Chat that they take part in
25. If you see it is their birthday via Facebook or LinkedIn, send them a birthday greeting on Twitter

---

Case Study: How Big Storms Led to a Big Change

EXPERT: MIKE TURNER

The problem

Two years ago, storms in the South West of England broke the railway line (yes, it literally broke) and cut off most communication to and from London.

In 2013, businessman Mike Turner had moved down to Cornwall, in the West Country, expecting to continue business as normal, traveling between London and Cornwall.

Every couple of weeks, he would travel up to London for two-and-a-half days of client meetings and run a networking club. In between, he did Skype coaching and Internet marketing with a partner in London, and his wife's franchise business was expanding as well. Then, at the beginning of February 2014, the railway line broke, and the only way to get to London was to spend five hours driving each way.

At the beginning of March, Mike got invited to speak at an event in Cornwall to talk in general about Social Media, and he also went to a local business expo. He decided to focus on building a local business.

'When we moved, I didn't have that intention at all, but it made me think that I know a fair bit about Social Media, and maybe that would be of use from a local perspective.

'I checked out the local competition, and there wasn't a lot, and the competition wasn't strong. The issue I had was that nobody knew me. Back in Sussex and London, I could trade off my name, but in Cornwall and Plymouth, nobody knew who I was.'

What he did

Mike's first priority was to raise his profile locally, and he would do that through a combination of networking and, in the first instance, using Twitter. After a while, he also used LinkedIn proactively.

FACE-TO-FACE NETWORKING

'Networking is a slow process of getting to meet various people in a new area. However, a fast route is to set up your own networking.

'I set out to do that and opened my first networking in June 2014; a simple Six O'clock Club. "Grab a drink and talk to people" type of networking. The type that happens in a bar after work. Coincidentally, on the 6th of the 6th at 6 O'clock, six people turned up. We ran another one a couple of weeks later, which had 16 people. Now, 18 months later, we regularly get 80 people coming to the Six O'clock Club.

'It's had an enormous effect on my profile in terms of who knows me, and who I know, in and around the Plymouth area by doing that one thing.'

FACEBOOK

Mike connected with people on Facebook as well as on Twitter and now has around 400 local connections on Facebook, but most of his profile-raising happened through Twitter.

TWITTER

This is a step by step guide to what he did on Twitter:

- He started by searching for people in business in and around Plymouth and who were influential. He looked for people who tweeted regularly and engaged on Twitter
- He looked at what people were doing and made Twitter lists of people in and around the Plymouth area. He watched the list to find the people who retweeted other people's stuff and, if those people were highly active, he engaged with them
- By following lots of local people, many people followed him back
- Then he started talking about the Six O'clock Club to the people on his Twitter lists
- He didn't talk specifically about his business
- He focused on content that would add value to local business people
- Quickly, his networking club grew and, by Christmas 2014, they had a Christmas party with about 120 people. All of those people had come, primarily, from Social Media and word of mouth
- Consistency is also important, and you need to maintain a presence either in person or by scheduling. For example, Mike regularly took part in Twitter chats or Business Hours on Twitter. Occasionally, when he couldn't attend, he would schedule Tweets saying, 'Hello #Plymouthhour how are you this evening?' Then would schedule one for halfway through and another one at the end, saying, 'Great Twitter hour, I'll catch up with you all over the next 24 hours', and then he would go back

and review the tweets on the hashtag and engage with Tweets at his leisure over the next 24 hours

- Mike started by manually adding all the people from Twitter chats to Twitter lists, but now automates this with IFTTT, which I told him how to do
- Mike describes Twitter hours as, 'A bunch of people that are active on Twitter and obviously want to promote their business, and all within a geographical area, or have a specific common interest'
- Mike recommends using lists whenever you find things in common between groups of people
- Mike uses Hootsuite scheduling prolifically. He schedules out the Six O'clock Club Tweets, as well as his offers

LINKEDIN

At the beginning of 2015, Mike started using LinkedIn more than he had done before.

Optimised profile

'I did all the right things and took the advice Nicky gave me in having my profile properly optimised, and with a decent picture, and filled in everything that I could possibly fill in on LinkedIn. I also did all the little things; for example, a summary at the top rather than the bottom.

'Then I did the classic LinkedIn things like going off and seeing who's there and who could introduce you to other people. Bearing in mind that I started from scratch here in the West Country, I didn't know a lot of people on LinkedIn, and all my contacts were elsewhere in the country or the world.'

Automated profile views

> *WARNING: Tread carefully if you choose to Automate Profile views on LinkedIn. There are a multitude of apps available, so I thought it important to include it in this book, even though they make me feel uncomfortable. LinkedIn will sometimes suspend accounts that use them, especially if they get reported. I know that some people do get results from doing it. Mike's initial results proved successful in the first months, but the tool no longer showed great results because he had probably connected to most of his ideal customers locally already.*

'With a simple Chrome extension, I automated the process of looking at other people's profiles. Using an advanced search criteria of looking for managing directors within 25 miles of Plymouth, will bring you back a search result that matches your criteria. You can either look through the profiles manually or use the Chrome extension to look at every one of those profiles consecutively for a set period of time.

'LinkedIn notifies those people that you have looked at their profile. People proactive on LinkedIn will look at the profiles of people who have viewed them.

'When they come and look at your profile, what they have is somebody that could, potentially, help them with Social Media management, marketing, coaching, and someone who knows a thing or two about those particular issues. This does two things:

'Firstly, they've looked at my profile and, as far as LinkedIn is concerned, that puts me up a notch because the more people looking at my profile, the higher I rank for views in people like you. This has a knock-on effect, I believe but can't prove this, because I have a relatively common name, including some famous Mike Turners, from football players to a congressman, and I'm competing with people who have lots of coverage. My LinkedIn profile appears on page one of Google, and we've tested it across the UK and with people in the States.

'The second thing is that people see what you do and then get in touch, saying that they are interested. I first started doing this in January 2015, and within two or three days, I had an enquiry that turned into a £500 (approximately $750) job. Not bad for $42 for the Chrome extension, and the 30 minutes it took to set it up. Over the course of that year, it accounted for over £5,000 worth of business.'

Results

At the start of 2014, Mike Turner did not have a business in his local area and worked from an office at the back of his house. He started to take on employees, and by the end of 2015, had moved into an office with six other people.

At the start of 2014, most of Mike's income was generated as a business coach exchanging time for money. He also sold Internet marketing products. He now has a Social Media Agency and his business is Marketing and Lead Generation. Most of the work he does now is campaign driven, or Social Media Management for businesses that don't have the time or skills to do it themselves.

His agency is listed 6th in the SMAUK list of 500 Social Media agencies in the UK. He is also in UK Entrepreneurs' top 100 most influential business founders in the UK on Social Media.

CHAPTER 9

Nurturing Relationships on Scale

How do you manage leads coming into your business? Do you use a mixture of business cards, emails, and notes on paper, maybe a spreadsheet, or a contact management system? If you started up your business, you probably would have developed a system that worked for you. The problem is that not all home-grown systems work when the business grows. If you have an ad-hoc approach to dealing with leads, you are certainly not alone, but maybe it is time to have a more structured system for dealing with the sales process.

The Dunbar number of 150 is the number of people with whom we can maintain relationships of trust. Due to our evolutionary biology, according to Robin Dunbar, our brains are hard-wired to be in communities of approximately 150. Generally, these communities would consist of family members, friends, and peers that we have met face-to-face and that we will remember names and details about their lives. I am sure we can all relate to forgetting people's names that we haven't seen for a while even though we used to socialise together. The Internet and Social Media have expanded the number of people we come into contact with dramatically, so we need to help our brains cope with maintaining and tracking relationships more effectively. Most small business owners don't use a software system to help them and rely on emails, spreadsheets, and calendar prompts.

Expert Tips on Nurturing Relationships on Scale

EXPERT: JON FERRARA

I thought it would be interesting to speak to Jon Ferrara, who created one of the first Customer Relationship Management (CRM) software programs called GoldMine back in the 80s. He is also the CEO of Nimble.com, a pioneering Social Sales and Marketing CRM that's affordable and integrates beautifully with Social Media. Jon Ferrara is a well-known Social Selling speaker and influencer, and I like what he has to say. But, mostly, I wanted to talk to him because I thought it would be useful for you to model someone used to managing multiple relationships on Social Media in a way that feels personal. As you read what he has to say, think about how you manage your relationships with your potential customers and influencers, and what you can do to improve it.

Jon Ferrara says, 'To understand how to use CRM, you need to know what it is, and a CRM for me and for most people is a fancy contact manager. It's a place for you to put the names of the people you're in contact with, log what you did, and log what you should do so that you can build relationships that drive measurable business results.'

Jon Ferrara recounted how, when he started in sales, they used to give him leads on a sheet of paper. He would cold call the leads and make notes on the piece of paper. He would then put his appointments in his leather Day Runner calendar and communicate with his team with pink while-you-were-out slips. He then did his forecasts separately on spreadsheets.

From Jon:

I thought the way sales people worked was broken. I knew a lot about computers and software back then. I bought my first computer in 1978 when I was 18 while studying Computer Science at a university working my way through school in sales at a computer store. I knew almost every single business software program known to mankind at the time (in the 1980s, there weren't more than a few hundred), and there wasn't a networkable relationship platform that unified contacts, email, and calendar activities with sales and marketing automation. Outlook didn't exist. Salesforce didn't exist. The terms CRM, SFA, and Marketing Automation did not exist.

So, I envisioned building a networkable business platform that could manage a whole team's interactions and conversations with prospects and customers. I had dreamed up this idea of GoldMine. At 29 years old, out of an apartment, and with two kids, we pioneered what we know of today as CRM.

But, in reality, CRM today isn't relationship management, its reporting management. In reality, most CRMs are not for relationships. They are for reporting on your sales people's activities. The reason they call it Salesforce is that you have to force sales people to use CRM!

The sales people have a CRM, and the marketing people have a marketing program, and the social people have a social dashboard, an accountant has an accounting program, and nobody talks to each other, and everybody lives in email in Outlook or Google Mail.

The sad truth is that out of 225 million global businesses, less than 1% use any CRM.

To most people, CRM is their email inbox, social media, or a spreadsheet. And our contact managers are broken because emails, contacts, and calendar activities are in three separate tabs.

The number one cause of failure of most CRMs is lack of use

You work for your CRM, it does not work for you. You have to Google somebody before a meeting, then you log what you know about the person and their company in the CRM. To build relationships, you engage prospects on whatever channel is effective for communicating with that person, like email and social, and then log what you did. You have to go to the contact tool or the CRM to log data and look data up.

The reality is that you shouldn't have to work for your CRM, it should work for you. You're a human being and we don't like to type things in computers. Most people don't log details about people or what the business is about or what they did or what they need to do.

Without automatic logging of emails, calendars, and social, you don't have the history of conversations and the interactions for you and the team. That's called context. Context is what happens before and what's going to happen next. Being able to see the context is important to:

- Understand how you might interact with that person
- Get insights into who they are and what they are about
- If they are connected to you or your team
- Be able to see what they have said about you, your team, or the brand

I truly believe that the more digital we get, the more human we need to be, and it's not B2B (Business to Business) or B2C (Business to Consumer), it's P2P (People to People). People buy from people, and they buy from people they like. And they like people who know them.

So, it is your job to know people and to figure out how you might serve them because, I think, that's why we're here.

The thing is that, today, conversations aren't just on email, they are wherever your customers have conversations such as Twitter, Facebook, LinkedIn, Pinterest, Instagram, Google Plus, Quora, and now Snapchat.

I think that is the future of relationship management, which is being able to get instant insights and context on anyone, anywhere, and to be able to add them to your relationship database, and then being able to do the things you need to do to follow-up and follow-through to connect.

It's inhumane to expect people to type in data. We don't do that.

The bottom line is that CRMs today are mainly used by salespeople for prospects and customers. The problem is that it's not just prospects and customers that you need to touch to grow your business. They need to connect with the influencers around your prospects and customers.

With Nimble, no matter where I work, I have this intelligent platform that will always give me the information about who people are and what is going on with them and our history. This will allow me to do the things that I need to do, the follow-up, and follow-through. Basically, no matter who is looking at me, I can easily bring up their record if they are in Nimble, or build their record with one click because it gives me instant profiles, and this works anywhere I am.

I can be sitting inside my dashboard and looking at this person talking to me or about me, and it is easy for me to hover and discover, to click and connect. Nimble is intelligent everywhere I work.

At Nimble, we can enter those bloggers, third-party investors, advisors, prospects, and customers, and it's not just sales people that touch them. Everybody in the company touches them.

In reality, we have no salespeople at Nimble, it's all (basically) prospects, customers, and care people, and everybody in a company should be sharing a Common Relationship Platform that gives you:

- The contact
- The history of interactions
- Email and
- Calendar for everybody and
- Insights into who that person is and what their business is about

So that when you connect to them, you understand who they are and how you might serve them.

Your relationship platform should work for you by building itself in the data account with email, calendar, and contacts. It should also match the social profiles, bring the data down, keep it up to date, and then work with you in any program you are in. So, no matter where you are, you have what you need to engage authentically and relevantly to earn that person's trust, and stay top-of-mind when they make a buying decision, so they think of you and regard you a friend.

What got me back into this business is that five years ago, I started to swim in the social river and saw its immense power. I saw it was going to change the way we work and play, and the way customers make buying decisions and where companies engage with them. I started to look for a relationship platform that enabled me to integrate social listening engagement to my contacts, and I couldn't find it.

Then I looked at CRM systems and saw that they weren't even about re-lationships and had no idea of social. They are about reporting. So, I had the same feeling with GoldMine, where I had a need and envisioned that many people would too, and I set about building it. The problem is that five years ago, most people had no idea what social was, and they thought that Facebook was a place to hook up with their high-school sweethearts, and that Twitter was a place to follow celebrities, and LinkedIn a place to get a job. Today, it changes the way we work and play.

I still remember how employers would lock employees out of a browser because they felt afraid they would waste time.

I think it is a mistake for business to engage with customers strictly on the identity of their company. Ultimately, what your consumer wants to know is if your business has a human entity. Does it have thought leaders crossing an entire company that they can engage with and build relationships? I think the future company brand is going to be built on the team member's brand, building their identities and sharing content to be-come trusted advisors and thought leaders, which then build the company brand.

If you want an example of that, you will see that IBM team members around the globe are sharing content, and building their brand as social business leaders, which in turn, builds the company brand.

Most people don't use a tenth of any of the CRMs they have

What they should want is something that enables them:

- To put in anybody their business comes in contact with
- To be able to track them
- To create a history of the interactions, emails, and calendar
- To map the profile of them and their company
- To bring the data down about them and their company
- Then use that database to segment the community around their business into the types of people they engage with. They may be customers, vendors, strategic relationships, and influencers of the customers

For example: Were I an investment advisor, I'd probably have relationships with accountants because they are the trusted advisor to the business person that I might want to advise.

So, you want this database of all these people, and then be able to use the database to segment who you should be connecting to, to do some nurture marketing, and measure that result. Then engage with the people in a human way to drive results, whether it's a sale or a recommendation, or them integrating with you.

In the pipeline that you create, the forecast may not always be a sale, but it is the result of a business goal.

Service is the new sale. The more people you can grow, the more you'll grow, and we need to stop talking about selling and talk about serving.

On a daily basis, connect to other business people and figure out how you can make them better, smarter, and faster. The world won't come to you.

(From the author: We spoke about different Social Media Networks. For Jon Ferrara, Twitter is more powerful than LinkedIn.)

More from Jon: 'Nimble told me that this guy, the Senior Vice President and GM of IBM's midmarket S&B group, had followed me on Twitter. I followed him back and sent him a DM saying, I'd love to get to know you. Let's connect for a phone call. He DM'd me his number 30 seconds later, and we had a call. Now, IBM is a business partner, all because I shared content that he saw. He engaged me, and I saw it and thanked him back. That would never happen on LinkedIn.'

Jon describes the way he thinks of different social platforms:

I think Twitter is like going for a walk with somebody, and LinkedIn is like going into their lobby. Facebook is like bringing them home for dinner, and Instagram is a way that you see somebody's heart and soul.

I think that if you want to connect with another human being, you need to share your heart and soul because that's how we build trust and intimacy.

For me, they all go hand in hand, and a picture tells a thousand words. Instagram is an easy way to see somebody. If you spend five seconds on my Instagram, you will know more about me than five minutes on my LinkedIn; at least the thing that you would need to do to have a deeper relationship with me.

If you share a little bit of your heart and soul where I see your mum and dad, or that your kids are scouts, or whatever it is, you open up who you are, and then that's a deeper relationship.

On Facebook, I have a huge number of business people, but we don't talk about business on Facebook, but rather about things that we're passionate about. Sometimes, people talk of political things, but most of the time, we talk about food, family, music, etc. Amazingly, if I want to reach out to another business person and send them an email, it's going to take longer before I get hold of them. But if I send them a Facebook message or DM, I can get hold of somebody in seconds; everybody is on Facebook.

So, if I'm doing a launch, I'd send you a Facebook message saying, 'Hey Nicky, I'm getting ready to release some new stuff that I'd like to share and get your feedback.'

This is the natural way to walk in somebody's digital footprint. I understand who they are, build a human relationship, and stay top-of-mind. That's why people need to be doing things other than LinkedIn.

You need to figure out ways to touch people from multiple angles and multiple ways to build a relationship, stay top-of-mind, and set yourself up as a trusted advisor. Then, when they or their friends make a buying decision, they think of you. That is the natural cycle of business because this is the way it's always been done.

If you go back a hundred years, this is the way smart people did business. Social just enables us to do it at a global scale.

- Share content
- Inspire and educate other people
- Set yourself up as a trusted advisor
- Stand out from the crowd

You will generate more signals than you can manage, so you will need a second brain because there is a limit to the number of people that you can manage in your brain at one time.

Thank you, Jon

Tips for Keeping Track

Practical Tools to Help you Nurture Relationships

LINKEDIN HAS A BUILT IN CRM SYSTEM

It may not be that sophisticated, but it can be useful. Everyone you are connected to can be tagged. You can also add notes to any connection that only you can see. Plus, you can set alarms to remind you to take a particular action. You'll find these in the relationship tab on your connection's profile.

Tagging allows you to:

- Filter your connections so that you can review only the people with a particular tag
- Add reminders about how you know the person to aid your memory

LinkedIn automatically tags people by the criteria (friend, colleague, etc.) you chose, or that they chose, when you connected. However, it is good practice to create your own tags, which allows you to add text to identify the connection.

- Tags can be up to 100 characters, including letters, numbers, and spaces
- You can add several tags to a person
- Up to 200 tags can be created
- The only person who can see your tags is you

Suggestions for Adding Tags:

- Where you met the person.—Event, networking group, online
- What type of relationship.—Customer, Prospect, fellow group member, friend, attended a course
- How well you know the person.—Acquaintance, good friend, not met yet
- How you met them.—Referral, Twitter, InMail

Tagging your connections helps you build relationships. It enables you to focus on a particular group of people that are important to you. It also helps you to remember details about people. If you are connecting with a large number of people through networking, there is a strong chance that you won't remember everyone.

Notes: It's good practice, when you have a conversation, to make notes. If you are not using a CRM system, LinkedIn is a good place to add it.

Reminders: You can set a reminder for a day, a week, and a month, or make it recurring.

CREATE A LISTENING DASHBOARD WITH TWITTER LISTS

I know we have already covered setting up a listening dashboard in the Discover section, and I've kept harping on about Twitter lists, but there is a strong reason for doing so. If you want to nurture relationships with particular people, you will need a process for doing so, otherwise, you will get distracted. Put simply, if people are of interest to you, it is worth putting them on a Twitter list so that you can find them again and can pay more attention to them. There is no point in creating lists unless you do something with them. You can remember to look at various lists from time to time, but you will probably find it more useful to put the lists into a dashboard such as Hootsuite or Tweetdeck. I thought it would be useful to include the following case study to show you how you can put this into practice.

Case Study: A Cheeky Tweet about Chocolate

EXPERT: ANGELA OTTERSON

Angela Otterson is a skilled Social Media Manager, who does Social Media on behalf of a number of clients. She creates Twitter Lists and uses Hootsuite to manage customer accounts.

'When I worked for a commercial laundry company, the objective was to build awareness in order to get new business in London. I actively followed London-based boutique hotels, restaurants, and chefs on Twitter in general. I particularly targeted the ones the laundry firm were interested in talking to by putting them on a list. I would retweet and comment on their posts, and over time, they started to respond and interact.

One day, a boutique hotel posted a picture of a room in which everything from the bed to flowers to curtains was made of chocolate. After retweeting and commenting about how yummy it looked, they responded that it tasted as good as it looked. I then posted that sleeping there might get a bit messy and that if they ever needed any help getting chocolate stains out of their bed sheets to get in touch. They retweeted that post and then sent a DM asking for contact details, which resulted in a meeting with my client.'

Keep a Record of Online Conversations

When you're interacting with people online, especially across several social networks, it is hard to keep track of where you spoke to a person. A useful tool for you to consider using is Digi.me. The free version allows you to archive all your Social Media activities for up to four accounts. One account is a Social Media profile like Twitter, LinkedIn, Facebook

Business Page, or Facebook Personal Profile. The premium version, which starts at £4.99 ($6.99) per year for four accounts, allows you to search for conversations and provides you with analytics, which is helpful for both nurturing relationships and measuring the results.

What this means is that you have a full record of your social interactions so that you can always go back and find anything you've said for reuse, or if you need it for compliance recording. You can search across your whole story to find ... well, anything you want—from when you posted an offer and who responded, to a tip or comment that someone left on your page, to a comment you made on one of your networks.

Insights (available on the premium versions) allow quick and valuable insights into your activity, including who you interact with most, and your most popular pictures and posts (retaining their original likes/comments). There are many things you can do here from the inbuilt analytics or getting spreadsheets of Follower data, for example, to manipulate yourself. For example: What your most popular post across the networks you use was over any specified timeframe, how your follower count has grown, and which people are no longer following you

The journal feature allows you to select any date and see what you posted across your platforms, while the flashback features tell you what you were doing on this date in the past, and makes ideal material for blog posts. The free version allows you to test the premium version for 30 days if you want to have a play.

Make Sure You Keep Track

Getting started

You need to make sure you keep track of your leads and where they came from and, if you are fostering relationships with new people, you want to keep notes of those too. If you already have a system in place, congratulations. But so many businesses don't do so in a systematic way. If you are solely responsible for new business, then you can get away with keeping your contacts on a spreadsheet or using your contacts in your email system. It is important to have a system of tracking conversations and actions that you need to take rather than trying to keep track of everything in your head. I know I've lost business by not following up on enquiries and proposals. It doesn't have to be super sophisticated or high-tech, but it needs to work for you.

Create an Excel spreadsheet, Google Doc, or download a free CRM spreadsheet from the Internet, whichever way works for you, but do get started. If you choose to use CRM software later, it is easy to upload the spreadsheet.

Choose software that works for you

There are many inexpensive CRM systems available. Make sure that it works for you. Ideally, you want a CRM system that integrates well with all your business processes. It is worth checking to see if you can integrate it with your accountancy software, your email marketing software, and your Social Media management software. There is no point in paying for a CRM system if you do not use it.

Hubspot offers a free CRM System.

Nimble has a free trial and is inexpensive and integrates with other online software.

If you are a Sage customer, Sage has CRM options.

If you are a Xero customer, Insightly integrates nicely. Insightly starts from free and the paid-for versions are affordable.

CHAPTER 10

Grow Your Email List for Nurture Marketing

L ead generation is the process of attracting qualified potential
customers and capturing their interest in your product or service.
The purpose is to develop a sales pipeline.

- On a simple level, a contact form on your website would be an
example of lead generation, or business cards collected at .an
Exhibition
- A slightly more complex example would be offering people an
incentive to sign up to your e-newsletter. You then send them
regular updates to nurture the relationship and, hopefully, useful
information. You use your newsletter to promote events, new
products, special offers, and promotions
- Or, on a complex level, you may have advertising campaigns to
lead traffic to a landing page with an offer and call to action. Once
people sign up, it triggers a whole marketing automation system,
which you have set up with a complicated flow chart of triggers
and IF and THEN statements. People will get different mailings
and options depending on what actions they take

Whichever way you work, traffic to your website is nice, but it doesn't
pay the bills unless you convert that traffic into sales. Obviously, if you
have a high converting website, and people phone or email you directly,

then that's great, but for most businesses, a large proportion of your website visitors will only visit once and leave without a trace.

It's worth creating what is often called a 'lead magnet'. This is a piece of content that your potential customers will find useful and helpful and that they can only access by submitting their email address. It could be an ebook, or as simple as a checklist. You would set up an automated sequence of emails so that, once people sign up for your Free Offer, they get nurtured before you go in with a sales pitch. A good lead magnet is something that your customers will genuinely feel has value, and that is suitable for the buying stage they are in.

Building a list by collecting email addresses is valuable to most businesses. You nurture the relationship with a potential customer by providing valuable content via email until they are ready to buy.

If you use email marketing in your business, you'll find it useful to add more people to your list.

How to Use Twitter to Generate Leads

Of course, you can use Twitter to drive traffic to a lead generation page on your website or a blog post with an ebook for them to download, but did you know that you can capture emails directly on Twitter? I thought it would be useful for you to know that you can capture emails using Twitter Cards.

So, what is a Twitter Card?

If you use Twitter, you will have come across Twitter Cards even if you didn't know that is what they are called. You will have noticed that some people have Tweets that are far more visible than the standard Tweet because they have pictures, videos, or text below them. These media-rich extensions to a Tweet are called Twitter cards.

Twitter Cards are More Useful than Images and Worth Using

There are two main ways to generate Twitter Cards:

- **Via Your Website.**—Every time someone Tweets a URL from your website (e.g., one of your blog posts), a Twitter card is automatically generated with an image of your choice. You need to add some plugins to your WordPress site to set up Twitter Cards, but it is well worth the trouble.
- **Via Twitter Ads.**—You will need to be set up as a Twitter advertiser to create Twitter Cards with an action button, but you don't need to spend money. There are different types of Twitter Cards, but for the sake of simplicity, I want to talk about the Lead Generation Twitter Card, which allows your customers to join your email database directly within Twitter with just two clicks.

Why You Want to Set Up a Lead Generation Twitter Card

It's an easy way to get someone to:

- Express their interest in a demonstration
- Subscribe to your newsletter
- Download an ebook
- Sign up for an e-course
- Access money-off vouchers or special discounts
- Download a cheat sheet
- Access brochures or leaflets automatically

The options are endless. And all of this directly on Twitter.

Pros of using the Lead Generation Twitter Card

- Make it easy for people to subscribe, download, and sign-up directly from Twitter, without leaving the platform
- People sign up by clicking on the button on the Twitter Card and one more click to confirm their subscription: no forms to fill, and no clicking away
- You have more than 140 characters to get your message across
- It contains an image, and Tweets with images get more engagement than those without an image
- They don't need to leave Twitter, which means you are less likely to lose them. You also don't need to learn how to set up a landing page
- Their Twitter name, email address, and username are automatically added without them having to type anything
- Easy way for small business owners to gather leads
- You can add people directly to your autoresponder
- Leads can be downloaded from Twitter as a CSV file
- You can send people to a 'Thank you' page after they have signed up
- You can reach a bigger audience with targeted advertising and, therefore, grow your list quicker

Cons of Using the Lead Generation Twitter Card

- Limited copy to convince people they want to sign up
- Limited image size to create an impact
- You can't drive people to a Landing Page, so your copy on your Tweet and Twitter Card needs to be good. (If you want to send people to a landing page, you would use a Twitter Website Conversion Card)
- You will be addressing people by their Twitter name once they've signed up
- May be less effective at lead generation than sending them to a squeeze page. You need to test this yourself

Tips for Setting Up Your Twitter Lead Generation Card

#1 MAKE EACH WORD COUNT

Guess what, with a Twitter Lead Generation Card, you have more than 140 characters to get your message across.

In addition to the Tweet, you get:

- A short summary (50 characters)
- An image to which you can add a text overlay
- Call to Action Button (20 characters)

Words make a difference; make each one count.

#2 ATTENTION GRABBING VISUAL

Every bit of research that I have read, as well as my experience of looking at Twitter Analytics on my Twitter account, shows the same thing: Tweets with images get more clicks, retweets, and engagement.

It is a no-brainer using visuals. Twitter Lead Generation Cards incorporate an image as part of the card. You can even overlay texts onto your pictures to get your message across strongly.

#3 TEST, TEST, TEST

Test, test, and test all the elements of your Twitter Card.

You can do this:

- For free by Tweeting a number of different options to your followers over a few days and see which one gets more interaction and leads (use Twitter Analytics to measure this as well as leads generated)

- Testing the same Tweet with different visuals/words or different Tweets with the same cards in a low-cost advertising campaign. Twitter suggests using 3 – 4 cards per campaign. You can see which card performs the best. When you know what works best, spend your money on your top performer

#4 BE CLEAR AND CONGRUENT

Make sure that all elements point customers in the same direction:

- Be congruent within all elements of your Twitter Card (short summary, image, and call to action) and your Tweet. It should be obvious what you want customers to do. You need to have one clear message
- Be congruent within Twitter by being conversational or offering valuable content so that your Tweet blends in with the Twitter feed rather than a direct sales pitch

#5 DELIVER

Remember, the sign-up is just the start of a relationship.

- Make sure that you integrate your Twitter Lead Card with your email marketing provider or CRM System; otherwise, you need to download the details from Twitter. Imagine what would happen if someone signs up, but then doesn't get any response from you because you haven't downloaded the information
- Make sure that it is clear what they can expect next. You can either do this in the 50 characters of the short description or send them to a thank you landing page after they have signed up, which explains what will happen next
- Make sure that what you deliver meets or surpasses their expectations and that you follow up on any leads generated

If you want to have a step-by-step guide to how to set up a Twitter Lead Generation Card, you will find it here:

http://www.nickykriel.com/blog/twitter/how-to-set-up-a-twitter-lead-generation-card/

Boosting Your Twitter Lead Generation Card

You don't have to spend a penny to use Twitter Cards:

You could schedule it to go out on a regular basis using something like Hootsuite

or

You could pin the Twitter Card to your Profile so that visitors to your profile see it as your top tweet.

but

You will get many more leads if you spend some advertising money to promote your Twitter Card to your targeted audience. You don't need to spend a fortune, and Twitter advertising is within any small business owners' budget. You can set up campaigns for just a few pounds or dollars.

You can target Twitter ads by:

- Geography—useful if your business is location-specific
- Gender
- Language
- Device—useful if you have an app
- Followers—you can target people who follow a competitor or someone in the same industry

- Interest—there are 350 categories to choose from. It depends on your business, of course, but it's worth seeing if some of these categories work for you
- Keywords—this is where Twitter advertising is so exciting because, if you know the phrases that customers who need your products would use, you can target those phrases or keywords. Remember, you need to put yourself in your customers' shoes; i.e., what would they say rather than marketing jargon? Is there a particular hashtag your customers might use? Is there a television programme that your audience would watch that has a hashtag? For example, if you are in Britain and have a bakery product, it would be useful to target people using #GBBO as they watch the 'Great British Bake Off' on television during summer
- Tailored Audience—you can target people already on your email list, or who have visited your website or a particular page on your website, or by Twitter Username

How to Use LinkedIn to Generate Leads

LinkedIn allows you to export all your contacts into a CSV or Excel worksheet. The data includes their email addresses, but this does not mean that you can import them to your email marketing list. Depending on which country you live in, a variety of regulations prohibit this. I know I have been added to some mailing lists this way. While you can contact your connections directly by email, LinkedIn is a great place to reach out to people because they can refer to your profile to find out more about you, it's like sending your CV with every message.

Ideas to get people to subscribe to your email list:

Connections - When people send you an invitation to connect, send them a message thanking them and ask simple questions to pre-qualify them. When they reply, you can offer your content and send them a link if your lead magnet is relevant. Make sure that it is something that has genuine value to them.

Customise your website links on LinkedIn - Customise one of the website links on your profile to take people to your sign-up offer. Make sure you call the link something obvious (refer to Optimising your Profile if you don't know how to do this, or contact me via LinkedIn or Twitter and I will show you). In your Summary, refer to your free resource and give them the URL. Tell them that there is a clickable link in your profile, or to contact you. URLs are not clickable in your summary, but most people will copy and paste links if they are interested.

LinkedIn Published Posts - LinkedIn Published posts allow clickable links. Write a juicy LinkedIn post that will encourage people to click on your link to sign up for the extra content. The benefit of publishing on LinkedIn is that you can share this content on Twitter and your other Social Media platforms.

LinkedIn Groups - If you have your own group, you can send a link offering something of value within your welcome message. Make sure that you personalise the standard response to any new request to join the group to include your offer. If you run your own group, you also have an option to add a website. You could use this link to go to a special offer landing page.

Search LinkedIn under groups for interests and join the groups—where, potentially, your customers might be:

- Become a good group member.—Spend a few weeks just adding comments to people's posts
- Benefits of comments.—You get seen as a valuable member and don't get flagged. It increases your visibility, your profile views, and opportunities to connect with other team members
- Different groups have different rules.—Make sure you get a feel for the etiquette for each group; i.e., some groups don't allow links at all, some won't allow links to your own content, and some don't mind. Make sure you follow the group's rules for links
- If a group allows you to share your content.—Then, after a few weeks of commenting and sharing other people's content, post your lead magnet content. Depending on the group, choose the most suitable way to do this; blog post with a sign-up form or Introductory post and a link to your lead generation page
- Share content.—Between 8 – 9 am ET to get included in the LinkedIn Daily Digest that group members get sent

SlideShare - The premium version of SlideShare will allow you to get people to subscribe to your list within the presentation. The advantage of doing this is that you get the benefits that people can sign up whether they have found your presentation on SlideShare, within your LinkedIn Profile, or shared in a post. A SlideShare presentation can also be shared on Facebook, Pinterest, and Twitter, or embedded in a blog post. It's also great to share within a LinkedIn group and is easy to create.

Part 4 - Convert

At some point, you need to take the relationships you have developed to the next stage. In this section we will be looking at converting conversations to customers by moving online connections offline.

CHAPTER 11

Convert Conversations to Customers

KNOWING THE DIFFERENCE BETWEEN A NIBBLE AND A BITE

Start by knowing what fish you want. If you don't mind what type of fish you're interested in, then it doesn't matter where you fish, what bait you use, or what hook. In fact, you are probably better off using a net than a line. But, for the sake of this analogy, let's assume that you do want to land a particular fish.

You would probably do your research on the best place to catch that fish, the best bait, and the best techniques. You may use Google to discover tips and local places, watch some YouTube videos, read a fishing magazine, and speak to a few keen fishermen.

When you go fishing, you want to fish where your type of fish is most likely to be. You wouldn't expect that fish just to jump into your hands. You need to take action. You wouldn't use a hook without bait or bait without a hook. You won't assume that you will catch a fish within a minute of casting your line. You need patience. A lot of patience.

Now comes the tricky part.

You feel something on the line. But is it just the water current? A nibble or a bite? If you reel in too quickly, you'll scare off the fish. But, if it is a bite, you want to start bringing it in. If you are new to fishing, you are in danger of reacting too soon.

Remember, you can't make a fish bite on the hook. You can be in the right place, have the right equipment, use the right bait, and use the right technique to increase your chances of catching a fish, but if the fish is not hungry or doesn't see your bait, it won't bite.

It is only when it's out of the water that you can see what you've got. It may be an old boot or a fish you didn't expect to catch, or it might be the right fish. The only way to find out if it is the right one is to pull it out of the water. The fish could still get away, but you are a lot closer to landing it than when it is in the water.

How would you measure how successful you were? Well, it probably seems obvious to you. If you were lucky and caught fish, you would look at the number of fish in total and what quantity was the 'right' fish, the size of fish, and how many got away. You would also evaluate that against the time you spent fishing and the cost of being there. And, you would make an assessment of what to stop doing, what to start doing, and what to continue doing.

Enough about fishing; let's talk about converting connections to customers.

Content, Conversations, and Conversions

EXPERT ADVICE: KEVIN THOMAS TULLY

Kevin has applied predictive analytics and data mining to the sales process for more than a decade to gain a strategic marketplace advantage for leading brands worldwide. In his current role as Vice President of Marketing Enablement for Markistry, Kevin drives sales and marketing enablement strategies and revenue growth throughout digitally-savvy organisations.

He is also capable of making the sales process sound simple, which I like. Initially, I met Kevin on Twitter, using the hashtag for a Google Hangout he had organised. As a special favour, he has created a flow diagram of his sales process for you to follow.

Kevin says:

'Customers are giving away buying signals for free on Social Media. Future customers are showing their purchase intent in plain sight when they:

- Ask questions that show their business needs
- Ask questions about issues in your industry
- Reveal intelligence about their business
- Reach out to peers for advice

'There are two types of buying signals to which one must listen: There are overt buying signals—when potential customers ask about prices or feedback about your product or the products of your competitors, and then there are covert buying signals where you have to do a bit of digging.'

As an example, Kevin suggested someone researching baby names. If your business sells baby products, you might set up a search term to monitor the phrase 'baby names'. This would indicate potential customers that you could place into a drip marketing campaign because they are likely to buy from you within the next year.

If people use buying phrases indicating intent, Kevin suggested approaching directly, but not with a sales pitch. He said that you need to think in soft touches. A sales pitch would be analogous to asking for marriage on the first date. You may know that your customer wants to buy, but your customer may not know that they want to buy yet even though they are sending out buying signals.

Kevin said that even skilled sales professionals sometimes lose sight of their selling ability when you put them in front of a computer. They don't realise the impact of the messages they send out because they don't stop to think what it would be like to receive that message. They recognise a buying signal from a potential customer and immediately launch into their sales pitch.

Kevin suggests connecting with potential customers and providing them with something of value, and preferably not content about your company.

'Help your potential customer with information that will guide them along their buying journey. Doing this will position you as a valuable resource for the information they seek, and it will keep you top-of-mind sometime in the future when they want to buy. It is selling by not selling. It's a much easier way to do business.

'Provide information and become a resource. Since the buyer is ultimately in control of the process, when your buyer is ready, the buyer will come to you.'

Kevin says that you can sell on Social Media, but you never want to pitch online. 'Selling creates a conversation. Pitching is saying "buy my product" to the potential customer long before you've established a relationship and earned the right to do so.'

Other than forgetting to provide value first, another big mistake many sales professionals make is that they forget to ask to take the conversation further into a discovery call.

Deeper discovery should always be done offline. Kevin suggests not to get into sales conversation online and to move conversation offline as soon as possible.

Kevin warned that, 'Many sales are lost because sales professionals don't do enough research prior to the discovery call.'

He recommended:

- Googling your client to find available data about them, their company, why they might be interested now, what they've bought in the past, and who they are working with
- Socially 'stalk' potential customers by looking up their presence on every Social Media platform, including their public posts on Facebook

He said that the idea is not to lead offline discovery conversations with any personal information you find online because that would be creepy, but the more information you have about a person, the easier it is to connect on a human-to-human level. He likened it to going into a client's office and scanning it for photographs or clues about a person's interests so that you can find something familiar to talk about to build rapport before you move into a sales conversation.

SUMMARY:

- Look and listen for buying signals
- Connect with people
- Provide useful content
- Have conversations to find out whether you need to provide more useful content, where they are in their buying journey, and when would be appropriate to move the conversation offline
- Suggest moving the conversation offline
- Research people thoroughly
- Have a discovery call

Thank you, Kevin.

Social Selling Flowchart

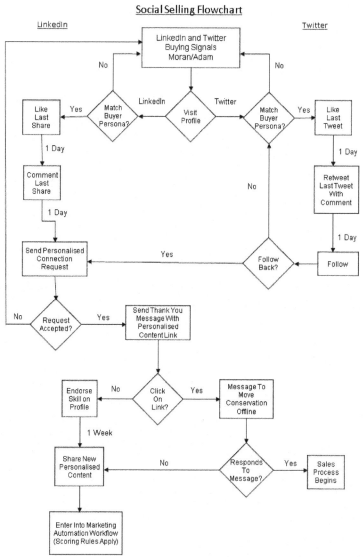

Social Selling Flowchart © Kevin Thomas Tully

Making Your Discovery Call

EXPERT ADVICE: THERESA DELGADO

Theresa Delgado has achieved her sales success in the highly regulated and extremely competitive pharmaceutical sales industry. Before she graduated from college, she knew that sales was for her. Throughout her 20+ years in sales, Theresa held various sales positions and one of her favourites was the position of Sales Trainer. Now she helps entrepreneurs, new to sales, how to communicate professionally and present to prospects and clients.

She believes that the reason a company succeeds or fails is because of the ability of the salesforce to be provided with the proper resources, and for upper management to manage and remove obstacles that prevent salespeople from doing what they do best. When you're an entrepreneur, the best way to succeed is to research, develop a plan, take action, and adjust as necessary. However, one of the most crucial skills that every entrepreneur must master to be successful is rapport.

Theresa is based in Los Angeles in California, and I met her through a LinkedIn Group. I asked Theresa if she would create a simple plan for business owners, who may not consider themselves as natural sales people, and give some tips for the offline conversations you will have with potential customers. Theresa created an excellent step-by-step guide to help you prepare for making the discovery call.

Theresa Delgado says: 'The first thing is that the discovery call is a conversation. You can't think of it as, "I want to sell you something right now". If your thought is, "I want to make sure that you're still my customer a year from now", you will have a completely different attitude.'

Theresa told me of a car salesman she knew, who was booked three weeks in advance for customers to come and see him to buy a car. Very unusual for a car salesperson! He would tell people that he wasn't just interested

222

in selling them a car today. He wanted to sell them their second and third cars. 'By having that attitude in the back of your head, it changes the dynamics of what you are trying to achieve.

'You can't sell everything to everybody if it is not a great fit. If you were to whittle it down to a certain specific type of person who would be the best person for your product, then they are going to have the best success. When you know they are looking for a solution that you can provide, they are excited because it is a great match. That's when they bring you referrals and talk to other people about you.'

Theresa Delgado is old-school about how she approaches the sales process: 'Get a piece of paper, write your list, and put reminders for yourself. With smartphones, it can't get any easier. I use lists and spreadsheets. I started in the days of writing notes, and that's how I like to do it. Alternatively, you could develop a contact list and write notes in the contact list section.'

Be aware of the buying cycle

'Remember, the bigger the commitment from the other person, the longer the process. If it is a big sale, then it will take you a few meetings, and also if your customer already has a contract with another vendor, they are unlikely to entertain bids at the time you start building relationships. Six months prior to their current contract expiring, begin developing your knowledge of their needs, challenges, and goals. When it's time to present your product to them, you have built a relationship and a strategy.'

Practice, practice, practice

'In the beginning, when you are first learning any new product or anything new, it is helpful to have a script to develop your features and your benefits.

- Record yourself on your phone and go through it, so you can see what you look and sound like. You can see your mannerisms, and you can hear the words that you are using: Are you going too fast? Going too slow? Are you using lot of filler words like "Um?"
- When you get more comfortable with what you have to say, it becomes natural because you've learned the information and know how to guide the sales call. It begins to look like a flowchart. You start at the beginning, and once you know that information, you can work through the points. Is it a yes or a no? If it's a no, then you go over here. That's when it starts to be more conversational

'But, in the beginning—for everybody, and it doesn't matter who you are or what you are selling—you have to have some type of structured format to learn.'

Research before the call

'Your goal is that your customer knows you have an idea of their challenges. By researching, you will ask educated questions. Researching prior allows you to maximise your time with the prospect.

'Do homework on the customer—the beauty of things being online means that we can do research, and that enables you to learn about the market. Even if you can't learn about specific details, learn about the market, go down to their geography, and see what that is like for them, such as the cities that they live in and who their customers are. Find out what their customers are like and what their challenges are, because part of your goal is to help your customer help their customer. If you can make them look good in their customers' eyes, that's a huge win and is why the research is important.'

Unlike the other people I interviewed, Theresa doesn't use LinkedIn as much for research.

'I can find more information on Twitter, Facebook, and sometimes Instagram than on LinkedIn.

'I was researching real estate agents at the end of last year, and it was very easy starting off on Twitter because everyone has their website on their Twitter profile. Then I could follow them to their website, and to their Facebook page. I could see what their challenges were easily because I knew what they should be doing but weren't. Then, you know how to get their attention.'

Theresa's suggested path:

- Do a search on Google and see what comes up
- Go to their Twitter feed and read what they post
- Observe what is interesting to them
- What conversations are they having?
- What hashtags are they using?
- Go to their website, make a note of what they blog about
- Are they are professional or 'trying hard'?
- Visit their business page on Facebook, what are they posting?

Tip for building rapport

If you research a group of people in the same industry, you will see patterns emerging, and it doesn't take you long at all. Theresa said that she had researched about 50 real estate agents over the course of two weeks, and it became obvious what the issues were for the industry.

Find websites that your target market would read. Study some of the key articles and pay close attention to the comments section. It is useful to learn what people comment. Look to see what they say, and pay attention to the words they use, so that you use the right terminology when you speak to your potential customer. If you are not using the same vocabulary, it shows that you are not familiar with their market.

The more that you can mirror their language and mannerisms, the more they will think, 'This person is like me,' instead of, 'This person does not understand my business.'

Think about useful visual aids

Sometimes, having a visual helps because you hit more senses when you speak. If you are meeting in person, don't talk from your visual; it conveys that you don't know your information. Instead, pick it up at the appropriate time, make your point, and then put it down and keep eye contact with your customer.

Objections (or concerns raised)

Believe it or not, objections are a good thing. Objections show that people are interested, that they are paying attention, and sometimes objections are smokescreens for another issue.

When an objection is raised:

- Acknowledge the objection. 'I can understand where you could be concerned'
- Answer the questions addressing that specific issue
- Always ask, 'Do you have any more questions?'
- Make certain that they completely understand the answer to their concern
- The mini-close for each objection is: Do they understand, and are they satisfied with how you are going to solve it?

Theresa likes to call them 'mini-closes' because they are little points throughout your presentation and conversation that you are getting their buy-in. You are saying, 'Do you see where this can help you?' and 'Do you see how this can make your process easier?'

You don't want to move along if they are stuck. Your prospect will not pay attention to anything else you say because they are stuck right here. Don't waste your time on the rest of the presentation until you break down the wall stopping them from moving forward.

Closing

A close is just getting someone to say, 'Okay, I will continue to talk with you.'

If you have done your job well, they will be ready to move to the next step when you get to the end of your discussion.

Think of the discovery call as an interview where you are selling your knowledge and skills. When you get to the end, you are ready to do your close. Sometimes, they beat you to it and say, 'What is our next step?' This is the biggest win, and you know you've had a great call.

You are building a relationship and getting them to go to the next step. For example, if you were talking to a friend and having a real good time, the close would be, 'Okay, let's go to lunch.'

A close is simply getting their commitment to move forward.

Step-by-Step Guide: Discovery Call

COURTESY OF THERESA DELGADO

Can be via Telephone, Skype, or in Person

- Goal: A sales call creates value and a commitment to move an opportunity forward

- Opening.—Thank for time, communicate agenda, and expectations—if the call is successful then ..., what else they want to discuss
- Discovery/Presentation.—Research dream client's business, prepare questions to ask—uncover needs/wants, prepare for objections
- Close.—Ask for business, gain commitment, follow-up action, next meeting

STEP 1: PREPARING FOR YOUR CALL

Preparing Ahead:

- Research and learn about the business of your client; this will avoid asking obvious questions
- Prepare questions to ask; have a plan to guide the conversation
- Prepare for objections by writing them down, and writing and practicing out loud your response

STEP 2: OPENING

How will your client benefit from meeting with you?

Preparing ahead:

- Why should your dream client agree to meet with you?
- How do you intend to create value for them during your sales interaction?
- Can you convey clearly what your dream client will get out of meeting with you?

What to do during the opening:

1. Thank them for their time
2. Set expectations for the call—'Today I am hoping to ...' (this helps when it comes time to end/close the call)
3. What else do they want to discuss?

STEP 3: DISCOVERY/PRESENTATION

What to ask during discovery:

1. What is their current experience with what they are using?
2. What do and don't they like?
3. What problems are they facing?

Listen to their answers and ask follow-up questions. Never assume.

Depending on the conversation, ask these questions; however, they might be better suited for the second call:

- If they're interested in your solution, when do they want to make a change?
- Who are the people involved in the decision-making process?
- What is the approval process?
- Will their current solution still work as their company grows or changes?
- If the client is not dissatisfied with their current situation, help them proactively find improvements that they don't yet know they need
- If the client is dissatisfied with their current situation, help them explore needs and determine what range of choices is available to them
- What is your dream client doing now that they could do differently that would produce a better result?
- What do I need to help my client understand about their risks, how to avoid them, and how to succeed with my solution?
- What proof will be necessary to create value for your client?

When objections come up:

1. Acknowledge
2. Answer
3. Confirm they are satisfied with answer (mini-close)

4. Ask if they have other questions, and if so, acknowledge, answer, mini-close
5. Continue with presentation

STEP 4: CLOSE

1. *How are you going to help?* (Your Client Expects that You Know How.)
2. Thank them for their time
3. Review the outcomes that you achieved together during that time; refer to the expectations made in your opening
4. Next steps.—Confirm any commitments that you made. Confirm your client's commitments

Ways to close the call:

'Thank you for being so open. I have learned a lot about your business and your challenges, and I have enough information to start working on some ideas.'

'Tomorrow, I will email you information regarding your questions.'

'I look forward to our next meeting. I'm available to meet again with you on {date and time} or {date and time}; which would be better for you?'

Depending on where you are in the sales cycle, the close isn't necessarily 'buy my thing.' The close is often 'I'm going to go and find you some information on these questions that you have, and let's set up an additional meeting to talk more about the specific topic.'

A close is just getting them to commit to the next step.

Thank you, Theresa.

Part 5 - Measure

How do you know if the time you're spending on Social Media is worthwhile or a waste of time? In this section we're going to look at measuring results.

Do You Track Your Numbers?

A few of you reading this will love keeping track of your numbers, and congratulations if you do! But, I suspect, more of you reading this don't pay enough attention to those numbers. If you are the type of person who hands your accountant your invoices in a plastic carrier bag, don't worry. This chapter is not to make you feel guilty but to help you think about your business numbers in a different way. I will keep this section as simple as possible to encourage as many of you as possible to start measuring so that you can make better decisions.

Ultimately, it's your bottom line that counts. Social Selling is not all about having nice conversations online, but about making those conversations count. And being able to measure that it counts.

CHAPTER 12

Measure what Matters

Now, contrary to what you may be expecting, I am not going to start with Social Media Metrics. Most of Social Media Metrics are geared toward the top and middle of the sales funnel metrics (I will explain what I mean by this in the next section). If you have an online product, you will be able to track the conversion rates and add values to your Social Media activities, but not everyone reading this book will generate all their revenue via online products.

In September 2015, the UK Government's Department of Business Innovation and Skills published research, which showed that while 98% of small businesses in the UK are online, only 28% sell goods and services online. The research also showed that businesses actively using the Internet to promote or sell, are almost twice as likely to grow.

I shall assume, for this chapter, that the bulk of your sales happen offline, and that you send your customers invoices by email or post. This chapter will also show you how to measure the effect of Social Media on your website traffic and conversions. We will cover:

- How metrics fit in with the consumer buying journey and your sales funnel
- Why you need to know the value of your customers, and how to calculate this
- Social Media Metrics made easy

- Using Google Analytics to measure conversions
- Twitter Analytics and other tools

How Metrics Fit into Your Sales Funnel

We've already looked at the Customer's Buying Journey in 'Nurture'. The classic sales funnel works along the same principles but operates from a selling perspective rather than a customer's experience. The terminology may be a little different.

Suspect—Prospect—Hot—Customer—Repeat Buyer

The idea is that you put a large number of people at the top of the funnel and take them through a process until a few of them buy at the bottom of the funnel.

When I looked for a simple model that I could use to illustrate Social Selling, I found a large range of different models with different processes. Some of them seemed so complicated that I think you would need days to figure them out. The problem with most funnels is that they imply that the sale is at the bottom. Often, repeat purchase, advocacy, and loyalty were an afterthought and represented by a thin line going back to the start.

What I wanted to create was a simple model, putting the buyer's journey, the sales funnel, and Social Media communication together, but also representing acquisition combined with retention, and this is the simplest way I can think of explaining it:

Top of the Funnel—Saying Hello

Action you take on Social Media:

- Attract new customers.
- Get attention with content and conversation that interests them.

Social Selling techniques:

- Personal Branding optimised for search
- Content that attracts attention
- Listening for opportunities
- Find potential customers
- Creating connections

Metrics that you use to measure at the top of the funnel:

- Number of connections
- Number of followers
- Click-through rates: Number of click-throughs to your website; clicks on Twitter Cards
- Impressions; i.e., number of people that see your posts
- Engagement rates: Interactions on your post: Did people click on the link, like, comment, or share it? The more interactions you have on each post, the more people are likely to see it
- Reach and Frequency: The number of unique people who saw your post and how many times

What you need to know:

- Not everyone you connect with on Social Media will buy from you, or wants to be sold to
- Not all your potential customers will be ready to buy when they meet you

- Traditional marketing methods work hand-in-hand with Social Media

Engagement style: Saying hello

Chatting, getting to know each other, finding out more.

Customer's buying journey: Awareness and Interest.

Sales funnel: Suspect to Prospect.

Middle of the Funnel—Getting to know each other

Action that you take on Social Media:

- Reassure Customers that you are the right person to do business with and that your product or services will solve their need.
- Nurture Relationships with potential customers, current customers, and influencers. Customers need to feel that they know, like, and trust you.

Social Selling techniques:

- Personal Branding as the Expert
- Content Marketing focused on helping the customer to answer questions as they are evaluating to drive them toward making a decision; case studies; sharing reviews
- Listening for mentions
- Monitoring key people so that you can engage with their content
- Nurturing relationships through conversation

Metrics that you use to measure middle of the funnel:

- Engagement—retweets, mentions, likes, comments, shares

- Profile views—tends to be a strong indicator that they are searching for someone like you
- Number of leads or people who sign up for your email list
- Number of enquiries by source; i.e., number of people who phone and email you asking for you to give them a quote or telephone call to discuss working together. It is important to know how they found out about you
- Number of InMails and messages from LinkedIn and Twitter asking to find out more
- Source of leads tracked online on your website
- Influencer Scores, which give you an indication of how effective you are—Klout, Kred, LinkedIn SSI
- Traffic to your website—length of time spent on site, number of pages clicked, pages visited, source of traffic, repeat visitors

Nurturing relationships—Social Media, email marketing, Customer Relations Manager (CRM), Contacts.

Engagement style: Answer and ask questions.

Customer buying journey: Evaluating options and making decisions.

Sales funnel: Prospect to Hot.

Bottom of the Funnel—Let's do business

Action that you take on Social Media:

- Make it Easy to buy.
- Make sure that the Customer Buying Experience is smooth.

Social Selling techniques:

- Conversion: Asking for the sale

- Discovery call (off-line)
- Closing the sale

Metrics to measure at the bottom of the funnel

- Revenue generated—number and value of purchases
- The cost of Acquisition (Customer Acquisition Cost)
- The source of the purchase
- Conversion Rate
- ROI per channel

Engagement style: Let's get down to business

Discovery Conversations and Closing the sale

Customer Buyer Journey: Action and Conversion

Sales funnel: Hot to Customer

After Sales—We Care about You

Action that you take on Social Media:

- Making your customer feel that you care about them.
- Retaining your customers. Building advocates that will talk positively about you, refer new customers, recommend you, and help your customers if they have a problem.

Social Selling technique:

- Nurture relationships through engaging, sharing, liking, or commenting to show you are paying attention
- Customer Care when your customer has a question or a problem

- Content—Consumer Generated Content, asking for reviews, recommendations, and feedback
- Keeping top-of-mind by conversations and content
- Listening for mentions from customers and responding

Measurement for after sales:

- Customer Retention Rate
- Lifetime Value of your customer
- Churn
- Number of Referrals
- Customer Reviews
- Number of Customer Complaints resolved
- Length of time to respond to customers

Engagement style: We already know each other, and I care about you as a person

Customer buying journey: Referral & Loyalty

Sales funnel: Customer to repeat buyer

How to Know the Value of Your Customers

EXPERT: BEN CHAI

I asked my friend, Ben Chai, to share his expertise about measuring the numbers that matter to a business. Ben has created financial wealth in a wide variety of industry sectors, namely, media, technology, security, real estate, and education. As a result of Ben's expert insight into how businesses operate, combined with a multi-faceted skillset, Ben has worked at director and c-level leadership in the areas of marketing, technology, operations, risk, and finance.

He has been responsible for the rapid creation of virtual teams to deliver projects effectively within emergency time scales and, against all odds, deliver projects within 'insanely impossible budgets, timescales, and challenges'. Through Ben's media companies, his books, podcasts, video-casts, and articles, Ben is globally recognised as an expert in matters of business, mind-set, media, real estate, Microsoft technology, and security.

Today, Ben's focus is in coaching and mentoring start-ups and entrepreneurs. You can read many of Ben's business articles on FiveYearsToFinancialFreedom.com

Here's what Ben Chai has to say:

When I first began in business, I was asked by a mentor how much it cost me to get a new customer. His question surprised me, and I replied, 'What do you mean? I had a few conversations with the customer, and he decided to give my company a trial order. So, I guess it cost me my time.'

My mentor looked at me strangely. 'It cost you a lot more than your time.' He smiled. 'The cost of your new customer is the culmination of all the work it has taken you to attract and convert him from an unknown to someone who will talk to you, to someone who will buy from you, and to someone who buys from you. That is the cost of your customer.'

'How much does it cost for you to keep your customer?' my mentor continued.

'Uh oh,' I replied. 'Perhaps we should have a drink, and you tell me more.'

His advice has kept me profitable throughout all the businesses I have run and sold. By knowing the cost of:

- Acquiring a new customer
- Retaining a customer so that they become a lifelong customer

I worked out who my best customers were and how much to spend on customer retention and customer acquisition. As a result of knowing these two costs, I was able to work out the lifelong value of a customer. More importantly, why in some instances I could lose money on the initial sales but, over the longer-term, make substantially more profit. The secret was to spend more time and resources in growing my relationship with my customers.

These two costs are important for any business. Very simply, if the cost of acquiring the customer is more than the profit made from the customer, then you will go out of business quickly. In the majority of industries, you will find that you can make more money from customers who already love your products and service. Businesses tend to spend far more on customer acquisition than customer retention.

Total customer acquisition costs

Your customer acquisition cost is the amount that it costs to find and convert an unknown person into a customer. If this cost is too high, compared to the amount spent by your customer, your business will quickly be in trouble. Add your customer acquisition costs together. (You can obtain most of these costs from your accountant or your expenditure printout.) Make sure you include the following:

1.   The salaries of any dedicated sales staff

2. All the costs associated with the sales person. For example, office space, office equipment, subsistence, travel
3. All the costs associated with the admin and sales support staff
4. All the costs associated with marketing and advertising
5. The costs associated with any other people who need to support this staff. This may be your time or a technical person
6. All the costs associated with your website and any brochures, case-studies, business cards, and other miscellaneous materials used in the sales process

The result is an approximate amount that it costs to acquire new customers. Most of these figures should already be with your accountants or your own cost calculations.

Customer acquisition cost

To work out your customer acquisition cost:

1. Work out how many new customers you've brought in for the year
2. Divide the result you got from the previous calculation by the total number of new customers you acquired for the year

First year customer profit value

The first year customer spend value is the 12-month income from all your new customers. You can get this amount from your invoice system. Out of the total income, work out the profit.

If the profit is less than your total customer acquisition cost, your business may be in bad shape and be living off its savings. A final indication of your business profitability will depend on the profit made from repeat customers, which leads us nicely on to the customer retention cost.

Total customer retention cost (expenditure)

A true and valid observation by many stalwart business people is that it costs substantially more to acquire a new customer than to keep an existing customer. So, it is worth spending as much as you can to keep the customer. Your customer retention costs are based around the same figures used to calculate your customer acquisitions costs.

The main difference is that these costs focus on keeping and servicing the customer. For example, you may have a sales support person for customer maintenance and a sales person for acquisition of new customers. The sales support person, traditionally, has a lower salary and is not commission based in the same way that the sales person is. You can quickly see that the salary difference alone results in a lower cost for customer retention than customer acquisition.

Note 1: If you are a fairly small (under five employees) business, here is a quick and dirty way to work out the retention cost. Take your sales acquisition costs and remove all the costs involved in marketing.

Note 2: In my smaller service businesses (under five employees), our business is focused on supporting 5 – 6 major customers and acquiring 1 – 2 new customers a year. In these businesses, our retention costs are actually higher than our acquisition costs. The reason for these higher costs is that we are working on lifetime values of 10 – 15 years. One customer has been with my educational business for over 22 years, spending a minimum of £60,000 a year, of which £50,000 is profit. You can see that with a lifetime value of 22 years, we have had a net income of over one million during that customer's lifetime.

Yearly retention profit

The yearly retention profit is calculated as follows:

1. Write down the total income per year from your existing customer base
2. Write down the amount of profit from that income. This figure is your yearly retention profit

It is important to get total profits for all the customers. Once you have the total, have your accountant or invoice software drill down and produce the yearly spend by individual customers.

If your total customer retention costs exceed your yearly retention profit, then your business could be in bad shape.

How to use customer retention and acquisition costs to become more profitable

In the majority of microbusinesses, customer retention is a substantial revenue stream and takes less finance and resource than to acquire a new customer. Essentially, you want to work on strategies that reduce customer acquisition costs and increase the lifetime of the customer by putting
substantially more effort into customer retention.

Once you know your customer acquisition costs and customer retention costs, compared to the profit made, you can quickly make:

- Decisions on which customers to hold onto and develop further
- Decisions on how much more to spend on developing existing customers

First, understand that we have vastly simplified our calculations. At a tech company I used to run, we had a customer who had the largest spend with us but was one of the lowest income generators once customer acquisition and customer retention costs were removed. However, this customer was important because the large orders helped increase our buying power, which enabled us to make larger profits on other customers.

Other customers that had substantially lower profit margins had a higher internal lifetime customer value because of their brand name. Their brand name was used as a case study on our website, which lowered our acquisition costs. The lowered acquisition costs were due to less resistance to buying when potential customers saw a brand name customer recommendation.

An important task for your business to undertake is to know the lifetime value, the acquisition cost, and the retention cost. Once you know these costs, your next tasks are to:

1. Create a strategy to decrease your acquisition cost whilst increasing your sales and marketing coverage at your target customer base
2. Create a strategy to increase your customer retention period
3. Create a customer retention strategy that would upsell your customers to other products you supply and, hence, increase the spend during the retention cycle

Here are several tips from the businesses I've run over the last three decades:

Tips to decrease your acquisition costs

*   Customer referral incentives. It is easier if a new customer comes to you via a recommendation than you having to spend time and money to convince someone to buy your services/products
*   Social Media recommendation. These recommendations are most effective from existing customers to their friends. I frequently pass on the details of people who have helped in my media and property businesses on several of the Facebook forums or privately on LinkedIn
*   Social Media education. Continual product education (not selling) on Social Media over a period of time is a low-cost way to acquire new customers

As a result of my regular posting of security podcasts, my company was offered:

- £100,000 contract to supply 60 hours of televised security education to a foreign country
- £40,000 contract to set up a security website for a software c ompany
- £20,000 contract to create 20 five-minute podcasts for a Fortune 500 company

Tips to increase your customer retention period

We shared earlier that it is possible to get more business from repeat customers. So, turn your repeat customers into loyal fans. Here are several techniques I've used and educated my team to do in their business careers:

- Personal customer value-add. This value add could be seeing a potential problem with your customer's business and showing your customer how they could reduce their costs and increase sales
- Birthday cards
- Seasonal cards not related to Christmas cards. Christmas cards get lost in the deluge of cards sent to businesses. Sending cards outside of this period, such as a Happy Chinese New Year card or a Happy Easter card, will make your business stand out. Always include personal notes in the cards
- Sending customers paper snippets on things that they are interested in or could help them in their personal lives. For example, one customer had a son who suffered badly from eczema; a rash that I also suffer from. It was no problem to share the journey I'd been through and some of the effective ways that have prevented eczema from persisting in my life
- Loyalty cards

Tips to use the retention period to upsell to your customers

Once you have a good rapport with your customers, tell them how other customers have benefitted from your products and services. For example, when you purchase an item from Amazon, Amazon also has a section that shows what customers of a specific book, film, or other item have also purchased. In addition, Amazon also has a section that shows other products from the manufacturer or books from the same author that you may be interested in.

Here are some other techniques:

- Advertorials within regular educational newsletters
- 30-day money-back guarantee on new product trials
- Social Media education campaigns that show how to get the most out of your products and what sister products support the existing suite best
- New product early bird special prices for one month only

SUMMARY

In this section, we've examined several financial numbers that provide you early warnings of business disaster, and how to leverage these numbers to double or triple your company profitability. In short, at any point in time:

1. Know your customer acquisition cost
2. Know how long your customer will stay with you (you know this by how often they buy from you)
3. Know your customer retention cost
4. Know the lifetime value (profit) of each of your customers and leverage
5. Have an evolving strategy to reduce the acquisition and retention costs
6. Have a strategy to increase your customer retention period

7. Have a strategy to increase the lifetime value of your customers by leveraging your service and product sales to existing customers

Thank you, Ben

Bottom Line Checklist

Here are some useful formulas:

Retention Rate

$$= \frac{(no.\,of\,customers\,at\,end\,of\,period - no.\,of\,new\,customers\,acquired\,during\,period)}{no.\,of\,customers\,at\,the\,start\,of\,period}$$

$\times\ 100$

Customer Acquisition Cost

$$= \frac{Costs\,for\,Marketing\,\&\,Sales\,including\,salaries\,\&\,overheads}{no.\,of\,new\,customers\,acquired\,during\,the\,period}$$

Customer Lifetime Value

$=$ *Annual profit contribution per customer x Average no. of years they remain a customer*

$-$ *The initial cost of customer aquisition*

Churn

$=$ *How many people stopped paying you for your product or services during the period*

Are you measuring the following?

- Number of incoming enquiries—how they came in and how they heard about you
- The value of sales
- Number of customers
- Source of the purchase
- Revenue generated—number of purchases and value of purchase
- The cost of acquisition (customer acquisition cost)
- ROI per channel
- Conversion rate for each step in your sales process
- Customer retention rate or churn
- Lifetime value of your customer
- Number of referrals
- Number of customer reviews
- Number of customer complaints resolved
- Length of time to respond to customers

Measuring Social Media Made Simple

There is a lot of talk about measuring Social Media ROI (Return on Investment). In fact, Social Media is scrutinized far more than any other marketing method. When I was preparing Social Media training for marketing managers for multinational companies, I asked how the ROI of their current marketing activities were being measured. I was told it wasn't. They said they were given a marketing budget. During a Social Media Strategy session, I asked the Public Relations (PR) company how their customers measured the ROI of PR. I was told that they didn't. As long as the businesses were getting media coverage, they were happy.

Social Media is not free

The platforms may be free, but the biggest cost of Social Media is your time (and your staff's time). You may choose to invest in tools (to save you time), and you may outsource generating content or even management, which all costs money. Time spent on Social Media can be wasted or well spent. Ultimately, you want to use your time as productively as possible.

Not all Social Media can be measured

There is a part of Social Media that will never appear in spreadsheets, and I will call that part 'The warm fuzzies'. People do business with people, and people remember the way you make them feel. It's the small gestures that build relationships. I doubt that any accountant can put a value on building rapport and trust, but you and I know that these things matter in business. Many business decisions are based on gut feelings. Every point of contact that your business has with your customer matters. Social Media is excellent for growing awareness and building relationships, and the value of this should not be undervalued.

Not all Social Media that can be measured will be measured

Even if you are using sophisticated measuring methods, much of the effect of Social Media won't be tracked. Did you know that 60% of sales occur after the fifth touch point? Often, only the last touch point is measured. Just a couple of illustrations of what I mean:

Recently, I had a message through LinkedIn from a new connection that there was a business tender that he thought I would be interested in. I was. I would have credited LinkedIn with the lead. However, when I met him, he told me that he had been following me for some time on Twitter, yet he had never interacted with me on there. So, was it Twitter or my credibility on LinkedIn?

One day, on Twitter, I was having a bit of banter with someone, who I think was deliberately trying to goad me about a blog I'd written a few years previously. I received a Direct Message on Twitter from someone saying that she was on my side. We had a few DMs, and then she asked if she could book me for a one-to-one online consultation. Score for Twitter, I thought. During our online consultation, she told me that she had been following me ever since she read my 'How to Twitter for Business Success' book over a year before, and how much she loved my blog posts. So, was it my book, my blog, the Tweets on the day, or all of it?

Just because the last touch point is the easiest to measure, it doesn't mean that all the value of the sale came from that single point of contact.

Saying all of that—Social Media can be Measured

One advantage that Social Media has over some traditional ways of marketing is that, because it is online, it can be tracked and measured. It is important to know what the different measurements mean so that you can use them to improve the effectiveness of your Social Media performance. Ideally, you want to get better results using less of your precious time. If you know what works, you can do more of it to get better results.

Social Media Metrics Demystified

Introduction to Twitter Analytics

Before we cover what the metrics mean, it would be useful for you to be familiar with Twitter Analytics. If you have never used Twitter Analytics before, you will need to visit their analytics website. You could Google 'Twitter Analytics' or go directly to https://analytics.twitter.com/. You'll only need to do this once. From then on, you will be able to find Analytics in the drop down menu when you click on your photo on Twitter.com.

I don't think Twitter makes it that obvious that there is more to Twitter Analytics than the home page. The writing is written in grey on light blue, right at the top. Twitter Analytics has five sections at the moment:

Home.—This gives you an overview of how you've done over the last 28 days, as well as the current month to date. It will also show you some useful overviews of your top Tweets and activities on your account. They call this your 'Tweet highlights'. Most of the descriptions are obvious, but I thought I would clarify these:

- Profile visits: Number of times users visited your profile page
- Mentions: Number of times your @username was mentioned in Tweets
- Tweets linking to you: Number of times your Twitter Cards from your website were Tweeted either by you or other people. You can set up Twitter Cards from your website so that, if anyone uses a URL from your blog, an image and description for your blog posts are shown on Twitter. The breakdown for each Twitter Card is shown in the 'More' tab

Tweets.—This is where you can work out how effective each of your Tweets are so that you can do more of what works. We will talk more about this in a bit. From this tab, you can download all your Twitter data to analyse it in more detail.

Audience.—Very interesting to find out more about your Twitter Followers in terms of demographics, interests, and location and more. This is incredibly useful to go through if you haven't looked at it before. Do your followers fit in with your ideal customer? You can't control who chooses to follow you, but you can control whom you follow and the content that you put out.

Events.—Not sure that this is particularly helpful. I know there is a section in Twitter Ads where you can target events, but to me, it is a bit meh. Let me know if you have any great inspirations.

More.—This is where you will be able to explore how your Twitter Cards are performing. If you haven't set up Twitter Cards yet, it is worth doing now. If you have a WordPress site, it is simple to do with plugins. You want to know if your actions are driving traffic to your website content.

Metrics when You are Building Your Audience

The numbers of followers and connections is a simple count of how many people have chosen to follow you on Twitter or connect or follow you on LinkedIn.

It is so easy to see how many followers you have on Twitter. Twitter Analytics will show you, in a graph, how your followers have grown as well, and give the actual numbers over a 28-day period or for the current month. It also shows if this has increased or decreased.

LinkedIn makes these numbers tricky to find on your profile once you have more than 500 connections. If you click to see who's viewed your profile, there are three tabs across. If you click on 'who's viewed your posts', you will see your followers. Followers are your connections plus people who have chosen to follow your post without connecting to you. If you click on 'how you rank for profile views', you will see the number of connections. The followers for your LinkedIn Company Page are easy to find.

- Don't be fooled into thinking that these are all potential customers or that everyone that you are connected with will pay attention to your every post
- Don't be fooled into thinking that someone with a high number of followers is more influential than someone with a lower number
- Not all your followers on Twitter will be real people; some of them will be bots trying to collect followers to sell
- Quality of connections is more important than quantity, but quantity does count. Low numbers can make you look as though you are new to the platform

Why you want to know your numbers

- You want to know that your audience is growing
- The greater the number, the better chance that your posts will be seen, and that your profile will be seen
- On Twitter, it is useful to keep an eye on your Follower vs. Following ratio. Ideally, you want to have more followers than you are following, but when you are actively building an audience by following people first, this won't be the case. Many people see people who follow very few people back as a bit snobby. Unless you're a celebrity, of course

Finding Out More about Your Followers and Connections

- Twitter Analytics breaks down your number of followers by demographics, which is incredibly useful. Make sure that you explore this to find out more about your followers
- You can find out more about followers on your LinkedIn Company website analytics
- You can find out more about the demographics of your LinkedIn Connections using advanced search

Metrics for Online Visibility

Or, how many people see what you post.

Impressions

Impressions=the number of views

Impressions are the number of people who actually see your updates in the timeline, search results, or from your profile. If you use a Twitter tool for measuring, your impressions will appear higher than they necessarily are because they will use your follower count as impressions, so use Twitter Analytics to get an accurate idea of how visible your posts are. LinkedIn uses an eye symbol to show impressions on published posts, and will show you how many views on particular posts. If you have a Company Page, I'm willing to bet that you will get higher impressions if you share the same post on your Personal Profile as an update. Test it out.

Reach:

$$\text{Reach} = \frac{Impressions}{Total\ followers} \times 100$$

Often, people will talk about the reach of a post, and it is expressed as a percentage.

(Strictly speaking, you should include all the followers of people who shared your post too.)

How many interactions for each post

There are a number of ways that people can interact with your updates:

- Clicks on image
- Clicks on video
- Clicks on links
- Clicks on Twitter Cards
- Shares
- Likes
- Comments
- Replies

All these interactions and clicks are also called Engagement.

Engagement rate

$$\text{Engagement rate} = \frac{No.of\ Interactions}{Impressions} \times 100$$

This is expressed as a percentage.

Why you want to know this

Engagement shows that an audience cares enough about what you are posting to respond to it. Which means it is potentially hitting the mark. The higher the engagement, generally, the better.

SOMETHING TO WATCH FOR:

It may be exciting to get a large number of retweets on Twitter, but ultimately, a click-through to your content is far more important. Make sure that you pay attention to your links. I've had a few tweets that have been retweeted a huge number of times by people with a lot of followers. I know that a well-meaning person instigated this. My impressions were exceptionally high for the tweet but, when I looked at the click-through rate on a link within the tweet, it was almost non-existent. There are sites where people will agree to retweet each other's content automatically. The retweets will add to your impressions and engagement, but offer no value to your business.

> *Tip: Spend time looking at the Tweets section of Twitter Analytics to analyse which types of Tweets give you the best results.*

Profile views

Twitter profile views are nice, but LinkedIn Profile views tend to be a stronger indicator of new leads. Profile views on LinkedIn show that people are searching for someone like you. Visit people viewing your profile. There is a good chance that they will approach you in the future. Where you rank in profile views, I believe, is a vanity metric, but pay attention to the number of people visiting your profile each day. Test your keywords and update your profile, and notice if it makes a difference.

Metrics to Measure Influence

There are a number of Influencer Scores, which you may have heard of, namely, Klout and Kred. Klout tends to get talked about a lot, and I believe it is important to know a few things about it.

Klout

Klout gives you a score based on your Social Media activities across a number of Social Media platforms. It's a measure of influence, but you need to take it with a pinch of salt. There are highly influential people in the real world with a low Klout score. There are also people who have a very high Klout score and have no real influence. Klout is not perfect, but it is useful for three reasons:

- *Firstly*, it is a guide for you to improve your Social Media activity. Klout score is based not only on how active you are, but more importantly, how much engagement each post gets. If you are just starting out, you would probably start with a score of about 15. It is encouraging to see your score increase. It gets harder to increase your score, the higher it is. You also need to be active on more platforms to get good results on Klout. It's easier to get a higher score if you are active on Twitter, LinkedIn, Facebook, Instagram, and Google+. If you are only active on LinkedIn and Twitter, your score is likely to be lower because Klout can't measure many of your LinkedIn activities
- *Secondly*, it helps you make an assessment about people you consider to be influential. Many people will follow people based on their Klout score. If someone has a low Klout score, they are less likely to be active on Social Media. So, if you wanted to find an influential blogger in your niche to talk about a product, it would be sensible to choose someone who has a higher Klout score. I would also be suspicious of someone claiming to be a Social Media expert with a score of less than 60. You can see people's Klout score on Hootsuite in their bio, and you can get a Chrome extension, which shows people's scores
- *Thirdly*, if you are interested in working with corporate clients, it may be important. Small business owners, generally, don't care about Klout score, but some corporates will use Klout for

Influencer Marketing and Employee Advocacy and may even expect recruits to have a certain score. You may not care about Klout, but you may be judged by yours

LinkedIn SSI

LinkedIn has created a Social Selling Index based on your activities on LinkedIn. You get a score out of 25 in the following categories:

- Establish your Professional Brand
- Find the right people
- Engage with Insights
- Build Relationships

It is worth seeing how LinkedIn ranks you, and if you can improve your score. It's updated daily. To find out your Social Selling Index (SSI) visit this site:

https://business.linkedin.com/sales-solutions/social-selling/the-social-selling-index-ssi

Metrics for Measuring Leads

It depends on your business what you consider to be a lead. It's important to track leads coming in, no matter where they come from, and assign a value to them. The obvious ones coming from Social Media will be via Twitter or LinkedIn. Obviously, if you run an account-specific promotion, it is easier to assess. Make sure that you count the number of leads or people that sign up for your email list. For the number of enquiries by channel, we will cover tracking leads online on your website next.

Track Traffic and Conversion with Google Analytics

EXPERT: ANDREA VAHL

Not only is Andrea Vahl the author of 'Facebook Marketing for Dummies', a top Social Media blogger, and Speaker, but she also runs an online Social Media Management school to train people how to run Social Media on behalf of clients. She knows great 'how to tips', and I love the way she is able to clear away the smoke-and-mirrors of Social Media and make things simple to understand.

I asked Andrea to share her advice for tracking the source of traffic to your website and measuring how effective Social Media was for converting into sales. I had my website person install Google Analytics for me years ago. Google Analytics itself is free. If you are technically minded, it is a simple process, but you may feel more comfortable getting someone to do it for you.

Andrea said: 'It is very important to measure Social Media because, if you don't know what is working and what is not working, you're going to keep doing some of the same things. You have to make sure that you understand what's really working with Social Media and do more of that.

'For small businesses who are just starting to measure Social Media, I think the big thing is to watch your Google Analytics, as one of the main parts of measuring. There are some great tools out there that can give you some comparisons, and you can compare the data within your Google Analytics. Google Analytics is definitely a big part of my strategy for measuring Social Media.'

Step 1: Install Google Analytics

If you are a WordPress user, Andrea says that it's very simple to set up.

'It can be as simple as using a Google Analytics Plugin that's available. That's easy to do, and it takes about two minutes to get it set up after you register. Go to www.google.com/analytics.

'You can also take that bit of code that you have for tracking and paste it into your website, either in your HTML or your WordPress theme, and get that started. It won't start tracking your traffic until you get that Google Analytics code or plugin on your website.'

Step 2: Keep your eye on the source of your website traffic

Not only is the total number of people coming to your website important, but you also want to know where people are coming from. Once you have some data, Andrea says, 'The first thing I would look at in particular is the traffic from social refers in the "Acquisitions" area. You'll notice that there are a couple of different areas on the side of the menu when you go into Google Analytics, and one is Acquisitions, and you can look at your social traffic there and see what is referring people to your site.

'One thing that was surprising for me when I first started looking at this is that I'm not a huge Pinterest user; I do a little bit, but I always forget to pin my post. But, I was getting a lot of traffic because other people were pinning my posts for me.

'So, it's important to know which Social Media platforms are driving traffic. When you see one that's doing well for you, think about how you can use those platforms and be strategic. Instagram doesn't have the links in the posts. It's only in either the ads or the profile, so you want to have a trackable link in your profile so that you know how many people are coming from Instagram.'

Step 3: Work out your sales process and how to track your sales

Accounting for the part of your revenue that was generated from your Social Media activities is important for calculating your ROI (Return on Investment).

Andrea says:

'Ultimately, most people want sales from Social Media, and that's great because we are not on these platforms for our health or to look at cat videos, but to actually generate revenue.

'You have to think how you're going to track all the touch points to get across to that end goal. With Social Media, there's a first touch or a last touch attribution to some of these sales.'

'What happens in practice is that someone finds you on Twitter and comes to your site, and maybe signs up for your email. If you're not tracking where they're coming from, later, when you send an email out about something for sale, and they buy, you'll see the email as doing the selling. That's the last touch that they receive, but it was, in fact, Twitter that assisted that sale and brought that person to you.

'So, you have to think about how you attract customers across all your channels. Keep those people separated in some way so that you know that they have come in originally from one of the social sites.'

Andrea told me that she is currently working with a dentist who is great at tracking down where the people have come from. They always ask people who contact them, 'Where did you see us? Did you see us through Facebook or a Facebook ad? Was it a referral? Sometimes, the hard thing is that people don't remember! They don't recall whether it was on a Facebook post or Twitter post or if they found you through a search on the Internet. If a friend on Facebook referred them, they are unlikely to say that that was via Social Media.

'What we're doing with the dentist in particular, and what I've done with dental offices in the past, is use ads to drive them to the website. We use some website retargeting so that we can reconnect with those people who come in through the ad. When they visit the site again, that shows a bit more interest. Facebook, Twitter, and Google ads have the capability to do that retargeting.'

The important thing is that at any point a new customer contacts you, ask them how they found you.

Another way that Andrea suggests you can measure sales is by using different coupon codes on different platforms. 'When you run a special promotion, you use a coupon code that is only available on different platforms. Create different codes for LinkedIn, Twitter, Facebook, and your email list. When customers redeem that coupon code, you know exactly where they came in from. I know some businesses will use different telephone numbers on different activities so that they can track the leads being generated from that source.'

Step 4: Set Google goals

Andrea says, 'You want to set up two things within Google Analytics that will help you track what people do on your website once they get there. It will also help track Social Media assisted behaviour for online purchases.

'Firstly, you want to set up some Google goals. These are easy to set up and are in your profile area of Google Analytics.

'A Google goal is either a page on your website that customers visit or how many pages they're consuming. So, it could be that if you want people to stay on your site longer, you could set one of those types of goals. If you are interested in the length of time they're on your site, maybe you have a goal to keep people there, and you want to measure how successful you are.

'Typically, people use Google goals for "Thank you" pages. This would be the page they end up at after going through a process of either opting into your newsletter or purchasing something. You would specify this URL as your Google goal. You can then see how often you convert traffic and be able to do a breakdown of where that traffic is from.

'Secondly, you need to set up UTM links.'

Step 5: Track conversion using Google UTM links

What is UTM code? It is a simple code that you can attach to a custom URL in order to track the source, medium, and campaign name. It enables Google Analytics to tell you how someone has found you online.

Andrea says, 'These are basically one of these long, extended links that tell you where people come in and what type of campaign it's associated with. You might have a particular initiative in a sales campaign, and you want to put in the source of Twitter and Facebook, and track which part of the campaign was most effective in getting someone to the "thank you" page.

'It takes a bit of work in setting those up because you have to create each special link ahead of the time that you are going to use them. I use a spreadsheet that has all of my links for my blogposts, website, opt-in pages, landing pages, sales, etc. I create all of these at one time and use them over and over throughout the campaign. So, if I'm Tweeting evergreen content out, I will use that code for Twitter, and I will use a separate code for Facebook. This means that I know which social site is most effective for me, and which is converting the most traffic into leads or sales.'

If you want to learn more about Social Media ROI, Andrea Vahl has kindly agreed to let you have access to some free training:

www.socialmediaroicourse.com/freetraining

Thank you, Andrea

In Conclusion

Now that you've read the book, what would you do differently? This book is all about taking action, and I hope that you have already started to take steps.

We've worked through creating a personal brand so that people feel that they know, like, and trust you, and sharing helpful content so that you attract the right person to you.

You now know how to listen for opportunities and find ideal customers, using search, but it is up to you to actually do it.

We have gone through making connections, turning strangers into acquaintances, and some of them into friends, business partners, advocates, and even customers. You'll enjoy Social Media so much more if you see it as having conversations with real people and, often, all it takes is saying hello.

Ultimately, you need to take some of those conversations forward and move them into sales, and I've shared insider tips from sales professionals on how to do that.

I hope you've committed to measuring the results so that you can make better decisions.

I would love to include your story in the next edition of this book, so I would love to hear about your successes, no matter how small.

I was thrilled that readers of 'How to Twitter for Business Success' sent me pictures of the book from around the world. From Cape Town to Cape Verdes, from Hawaii to Singapore, and from a hot-air balloon to an underwater picture. What an adventurous group of people they are. I would love to see where you take this book.

And, more importantly, where you take your business.

Make sure to connect with me on Twitter and LinkedIn.

Nicky

enquiries@nickykriel.com

www.nickykriel.com

ABOUT THE AUTHOR

Author Photo by Ingrid Weel Photography

Nicky Kriel is Social Media Trainer, Speaker, and Author of the bestselling book 'How to Twitter for Business Success'. Recently ranked in the top 10 UK marketing influencers on Social Media, she has been featured in the Guardian and the Daily Telegraph and is regularly interviewed as an expert in Social Media. Nicky Kriel specialises in Social Media Strategy. She has a background in Corporate Marketing and Sales. She is also Master NLP (Neuro Linguistic Practitioner) and communicating is her strength. Since starting Social Media training in 2010, she has worked with over a thousand Small and Medium-sized business owners as well as multinationals. Jargon is kept to the minimum, with the focus being on practical advice, top tips, and guidance.

When Nicky is not writing about Social Media, you'll find her wandering around the beautiful English countryside near her home in Guildford or having an adventure travelling around the world.

ACKNOWLEDGEMENTS

Thank you

TO MY LOVELY KICKSTARTER BACKERS

I was thrilled by all the support for my successful Kickstarter campaign. It really made a difference. Thank you to everyone who backed the campaign. The following people backed me at a high reward level.

Shelley Röstlund - Social Intelligence - www.mysocialintelligence.com
Paul Hookham - The Really Caring 60+ Recruitment Company - www.trcrc.com
Tom Evans - Author, philanthropist, podcast host - www.tomevans.co
Kathy Brown - Discovery Games UK - www.discoverygamesuk.com
Tim Bracher – WellbriX - www.wellbrix.com
Amanda Weller - Quantum Being - www.quantumbeing.co.uk
Julie Ruth - Loka Creative - www.lokacreative.com
Jane C Woods - Changing People-Gender Equality - www.changingpeople.co.uk
Jeri Limited - Bespoke System Development - www.jerilimited.co.uk
Steve Sapseid - BME Solutions - www.bmesol.com
Joanna Michael - Car Service Direct Ltd -.www.carservicedirect.com
Doug New.-.Infin8 Vision - www.dougnew.com
Nicola Trett.- FLOW Business Ltd - www.flowbusiness.uk
Joanne McGowan - Guildford Business Hub - www.businesshubs.org/guildford
Jack E. Traver Jr. - Traver IDC - www.traveridc.com
Thom Gibbons - Babba Ltd - www.babba.rocks
Shona Easton.-Stylish designed handbags - www.eastondesignstudio.com
Jackie Elton.-.Social Media Lincs -.www.socialmedialincs.co.uk
Felicity Dwyer -.The Heart of Work Career Coaching -.www.heartofwork.co.uk

Sarah Fenelon -.Director, Oraculum Recruitment -.www.oraculum.co.uk/
Rebecca Newenham.-.Get Ahead VA - www.getaheadva.com
Narn - Twitter.com/tweetingbyhand
Ian Taylor Taylor Commercial Repairs Ltd www.taylor-commercials.co.uk
Louise Hall Ervin Hall Ltd Affordable & accessible legal support for SMEs
www.ervinhall.co.uk
Cathy Carmody
Cornelis de Maijer
Natasha Fleming
Ben Chai - www.fiveyearstofinancialreedom.com
Dr Martin Stillman Jones - Venture Strategy
www.venturestrategypartnership.com/
Julie Bishop - JobHop - http://jobhop.co.uk/
Tim Fuell - Jibba Jabba - www.jibbajabbapods.com/

Thank you

There are so many people who helped me along my journey towards getting this book published, from people who gave me helpful advice to people who painstakingly proofread the book from cover to cover. A big thank you to all of you.

A special thank you to Lisa Kriel, Dani Maimone, Angela Otterson, Tracey Meade and Christina.DiCamillo

And to my lovely daughter, Natasha Murwill who produced all the pdfs and checklists as a resource for www.nickykriel.com/freeresources

Thank you to my copy editor, Harmony Kent.

I also like to thank Chris Towndrow of London Corporate Media for producing the Kickstarter video for me.

Thank you.

About the contributors

Stuart L. Morris

Professional Entrepreneur
Website: http://www.tricerion.com/
LinkedIn: https://www.linkedin.com/in/stuartlmorris
Twitter: @stuartlmorris
Stuart is an avid entrepreneur, trainer of entrepreneurs, teacher and tech inventor. He has a passion to see people lifted out of poverty by building sustainable businesses and has been involved in highly successful entrepreneurship projects in Moldova, Kazakhstan, Turkey, and the UK. He has been involved with tech inventions for groups such as police forces, military, hospitals, airports and many businesses since he was 14. He holds several patents in user identification and Internet security. His desire to pass on what he has learned from his experiences, led him to teach Entrepreneurship at Henley Business School and other universities in Europe. He also is a qualified paramotor pilot, self-confessed geek and father of three.

Dee Blick

Bestselling Author of Marketing for Small Business books
Website: http://www.themarketinggym.org/
LinkedIn: https://www.linkedin.com/in/creativemarketer
Twitter: @deeblick
Dee Blick is a Fellow of the Chartered Institute of Marketing (CIM), and has 30 years' marketing experience gained working with blue chip organisations and SMEs. She has a track record of planning and delivering successful campaigns generating £10 million plus sales on a shoestring budget. An award-winning writer, she is also the author of the Number 1 bestselling, highest reader review rated marketing book on Amazon - The Ultimate Small Business Marketing Book (currently 164 5 star reviews) - which is being released in China and Australia due to its tremendous success in the UK. Dee's third

book, The 15 Essential Marketing Masterclasses for Your Small Business, has been endorsed by CIM and won Talk Magazine's Best Business Award 2013.

Peter Springett

Content Marketing Expert
Instagram: @peterspringett
LinkedIn: https://www.linkedin.com/in/peterspringett1
Twitter: @PeterSpringett
Peter is the founder of Bright Content, a business dedicated to helping clients maximize the reach and value of their content through Social Media and employee advocacy. He has led content teams serving some of the biggest global names in the technology industry. He said that he likes to think of Content Marketing as a cycle.

Alan Donegan

Founder of Pop Up Business School and Enjoy Presenting
Website: http://www.popupbusinessschool.co.uk/
LinkedIn: https://www.linkedin.com/in/alandonegan
Twitter: @AlanDonegan
Alan Donegan is one of the Co-Founders of the Pop-Up Business School which has helped hundreds of new businesses start up over the last three years. They have helped people get their first client inside two days all the way to making £100,000+ inside the first year. He also runs a training business which helps executives, business owners and ordinary people all over the world feel comfortable when speaking to others, to inspire, enthuse and motivate through words and help companies to sell more of their products with their presentations. Alan has been making money for himself since he was age 11 - and still enjoys playing with Lego.

Mike Turner

Social Media Expert
Website: http://tindigital.com/
LinkedIn: https://www.linkedin.com/in/miketurneruk
Twitter: @michaelturner
Performance Driven Social Media Marketing. Facebook Specialists. Lead Generation, Coaching, Training and Management. Powered by Cornish Beer and Pasties

Jon Ferrara

Pioneer and Creator of CRM, Social Selling Expert
Website: http://www.nimble.com/
LinkedIn: https://www.linkedin.com/in/jonvferrara

Twitter: @Jon_Ferrara

Jon is a CRM and Relationship Management entrepreneur and noted speaker about Social Media's effects on Sales and Marketing. His most recent venture is Nimble.com, has re imagined CRM with by building a Simply Smarter Social Sales and Marketing platform. It is the first CRM that works for you by building and updating contact data for you, then works with you, everywhere you work. Ferrara is best known as the co-founder of GoldMine Software Corp, one of the early pioneers in the Sales Force Automation (SFA) and Customer Relationship Management (CRM) software categories for Small to Medium sized Businesses (SMBs). He has recently been recognized on Forbes as one of the "Top 10 Social Salespeople in the World".

Kevin Thomas Tully

Social Selling Expert
Website: http://www.kevinthomastully.com/
LinkedIn: https://www.linkedin.com/in/kevinthomastully
Twitter: @kevinttully

Kevin Thomas Tully is a globally-recognized Social Selling and Big Data influencer and strategist who employed the principles of Social Selling long before the term entered the popular business vernacular. A Johns Hopkins-trained scientist, Kevin has applied predictive analytics and data mining to the sales process for more than a decade to gain a strategic marketplace advantage for leading brands worldwide. With a C-level background in Sales, Marketing, and PR, Kevin has built multi-million dollar sales infrastructures and trainedaward-winning sales teams across variable verticals both as an entrepreneur and corporate officer. In his current role as Founder and CEO of ScealCom, Kevin drives sales and marketing enablement strategies and revenue growth throughout digitally-savvy organizations.

Theresa Delgado

Sales Training Expert, Founder of "Building Rapport like a Pro"
Website: www. TheresaDelgado.com
LinkedIn: https://www.linkedin.com/in/theresadelgado
Twitter: @TheresaDelgado

Theresa Delgado achieved her sales success in the highly regulated and extremely competitive pharmaceutical sales industry. Now she helps entrepreneurs, new to sales, how to professionally communicate and present to prospects and clients. She believes that one of the most crucial skills that every entrepreneur must master to be successful is rapport. To help entrepreneurs develop the foundation of this skill and build rapport with their clients and business contacts, Theresa has created the unique course, "Building Rapport like a Pro." Theresa has taken her knowledge and experience and created an extensive library for entrepreneurs to learn many of the necessary skills it takes to be a successful salesperson. You will find the "Building Rapport like a Pro" course and other sales tools, tips, and tutorials on her website.

Ben Chai

Entrepreneur
Website: www.FiveYearsToFinancialFreedom.com
LinkedIn: https://www.linkedin.com/in/chaiben
Twitter: @BenInSightChai

Ben is a unique individual who is able to think beyond the confines of conventional thinking. His 'out of the box' perspective, has helped Ben to create financial wealth in media, technology, security, real estate, and education. As a result of Ben's expert insight in how businesses operate combined with a multi-faceted skillset, Ben has worked at director and c-level leadership in the areas of marketing, technology, operations, risk, and finance. He has been responsible for the rapid creation of virtual teams to effectively deliver projects within emergency time scales and against all odds deliver projects within 'insanely impossible budgets, timescales and challenges'.

Through Ben's media companies, his books, podcasts, videocasts, and articles, Ben is globally recognised as an expert in matters of business, mindset, media, real estate, Microsoft technology, and security. Today Ben's focus is in coaching and mentorship techniques. These techniques have already helped many to grow and create successful businesses. You can read many of Ben's business articles on FiveYearsToFinancialFreedom.com

Andrea Vahl

Social Media Consultant, Speaker and Author also known as "Grandma Mary"
Website: www.andreavahl.com
LinkedIn: https://www.linkedin.com/in/andreavahl
Twitter: @AndreaVahl

Andrea Vahl is a Social Media Consultant and Speaker who is passionate about helping businesses understand and leverage the power of social media to actually grow their business. Andrea is the co-author of Facebook Marketing All-in-One for Dummies and was the Community Manager for Social Media Examiner, for over 2 years. She also uses her Improv comedy skills to blog as a slightly cranky character, Grandma Mary.

She is the lead teacher at FBInfluence an online Facebook Marketing Training program used by over 20,000 students and the co-founder of Social Media Manager School.

Andrea Vahl's proven ability to make social media marketing easy to understand and implement has directly impacted the bottom line of thousands of companies through her training and one-on-one consulting. Learn more about Andrea's books, resources, and get her Quick Start Guide to Social Media for Business on her website.

Herve G-Werty

Illustrator

Website: http://www.mutton-press.com

LinkedIn: https://www.linkedin.com/in/hervegwery

Twitter: @HERVEGW

Herve G Wery started his career as an architect, and then moved his focus to design and film making. A French national, he now lives and works in west Cornwall.

Herve's divorce was a catalyst for his latest project, which aims to help families, particularly children, cope with separation, any kind of separation. Divorce, Separation: Love your Children no Matter What ...

For most people this means the end of love. For Herve, his love story did not end with his divorce, because the love he and his ex-wife shared for their daughter remained

David Sewell

Book cover designer

Website: http://afflatus.co.uk/

LinkedIn: https://www.linkedin.com/company/afflatus-limited

Twitter: https://twitter.com/AfflatusDesign

David Sewell has over a quarter of a century of experience in the creative industry. Having gained his qualifications in graphic design with merit, David started out as an airbrush illustrator and art director in an advertising agency, coming up with concepts and visuals for campaigns, as well as producing artwork for print and retouching photographs. At that time, all work was done by hand.

Of course, most work is done on computers these days and in fact David has trained staff for several clients in design processes and artworking skills using Adobe products on the Mac. David's main areas of work include logo design & typography, magazine design & layout, design & artwork for advertising, branding, packaging and publishing. David also designed the first UK banknote hologram for the £20 note... and no, he didn't get any free samples.

I would also like to thank the following people for contributing to the book

Ingrid Weel

Author Photographer
Website: http://www.ingridweel.com/
LinkedIn: https://www.linkedin.com/in/ingridweel
Twitter: @ingridweel
Imaginative and energetic photographer & company director of Ingrid Weel Media Ltd. Social and Corporate photographer of people. Sci-fi geek, wine lover, a bit of a thing for bumble bees and yoga....

Andy Foote

LinkedIn Expert
Website: https://www.linkedinsights.com/
LinkedIn: https://www.linkedin.com/in/linkedinsights
Twitter: @andyxfoote
Andy has been a Teacher, Recruiter, Lawyer and Stay-at-home Father. He currently teach people and organizations how to use LinkedIn for professional success. A few personal traits: endless curiosity, a desire to share, attention to detail and well-honed people and networking skills.

Gerry Moran

Content Marketing Strategist
Website: https://marketingthink.com/
LinkedIn: https://www.linkedin.com/in/gerrymoran
Twitter: @GerryMoran
Global Social Media & Content Leader | Digital Dot Connecter | Speaker | Content Marketing Strategist | Visual Storyteller | Springsteen & craft beer geek

Angela Otterson

Social Media Manager Extraordinaire
LinkedIn: https://www.linkedin.com/in/angelaotterson
Twitter: @angelaotterson
Social Media Manager for SME's in Surrey, Twitter, LinkedIn, Facebook, Instagram, Google+ Pinterest. Reliable, saving busy business owners time.

Lightning Source UK Ltd.
Milton Keynes UK
UKOW06f0030071016

284621UK00001B/206/P